in clear, easy-to-understand directions. Just some of the many guidelines you receive are:

- **how to effortlessly prepare and install the "MBO System" in your school**
- **how to conduct a needs assessment program to identify priorities**
- **how to involve the total staff and get true participatory management**
- **how to conduct management review conferences for easier evaluations**
- **how to use the sample forms, written objectives, and time-phased action steps included in the book to aid you in implementing the MBO approach**

What's more, you receive practical guidelines for dealing with the many diverse human problems that affect your staff, letting you make them more results oriented and performance conscious.

A Performance Accountability System for School Administrators

A Performance
Accountability System
for School Administrators

Terrel H. Bell

Parker Publishing Company, Inc., West Nyack, N.Y.

LB
2805
.B35

Library of Congress Cataloging in Publication Data

Bell, Terrel Howard
  A performance accountability system for school
administrators.

  1. Educational accountability. 2. School
management and organization. I. Title.
LB2805.B35   379'.15   74-1357
ISBN 0-13-657189-1

Printed in the United States of America

To

Betty Ruth
Mark
Warren
Glenn
Peter

The Value of School
Management by Objectives —
and What It Can Mean to You

There are a variety of significant benefits that result from school management by objectives, but one is paramount in importance: it provides a proven, systematic approach to educational accountability.

This book deals with key factors necessary for a successful MBO system and how you can apply them most effectively. It describes a practical and *proven* system of results-oriented management techniques that will enable you to accomplish important objectives throughout an annual MBO cycle. The guidelines are presented with the experienced, front line school administrator in mind. In the fullest sense, it is a how-to book for those who have had little or no previous experience or training in using one of the most modern management systems in education today.

Public concern for better management and improved performance in our schools is reflected in the focus that has been brought to bear on educational accountability. The central idea of accountability in education is based on the proposition that a much more effective educational system emerges when outputs and objectives are more carefully planned and evaluated.

For example, school management by objectives helps to insure that the planning and execution of all school operations become universally understood by *all* staff members and admin-

istrators. The MBO system is designed to help any school administrative team identify and focus on their most important objectives. Once these have been identified and agreement reached,
it is infinitely easier to bring about the necessary forms of progress. The system is particularly valuable in promoting participative management in education.

When MBO is properly implemented with the active involvement of staff in fixing priorities and setting goals, it creates a new
sense of unity and teamwork throughout the institution it serves.
It becomes, without question, the principal tool through which
educational progress is attained. This system of results-oriented
management assures the administrative staff that the most critical problems are being met with detailed, time-phased action
steps that bring about practical solutions to important problems.

I observed the impact of an MBO system on the United
States Office of Education during the time I served as Acting
U.S. Commissioner of Education and Deputy Commissioner.
From this experience in the learning and implementation phase
of the Office of Education MBO system I became convinced
that this entire procedure could easily be adapted to the operational planning and management programs of school systems
throughout the country. At the first opportunity, I developed
actual experience in installing such a system in a school district
with 63,000 students and 72 schools. This experience, plus direct
activities with other schools that have successfully installed MBO
systems, has convinced me that both small and large educational
organizations have much to gain by the application of this proven
method of effective management.

In the early chapters you will recognize not only the urgent
need but also the basic fundamentals involved in this program.
It will become apparent that this system not only leads to personal
administrative progress but in addition brings about the basis
for increased learning activity in the schools. Later chapters
focus on the most effective ways to establish operational objectives and performance priorities. Operational planning, management and execution of action-step plans are covered in subse-

quent chapters, along with ways to involve the staff and the role of each member of the team. In short, this book provides all the practical information you will need in order to develop an extraordinarily successful program of School Management by Objectives.

Terrel H. Bell

Table of Contents

13

Appendix B *(cont.)*

A Performance Accountability System for School Administrators

1
School and College
Management by Objectives:
Keys to Performance
Accountability

In this chapter the need for a management system is explained. A brief overview of what a system of management by objectives will do to keep educational institutions involved in self-renewal as problem-solving organizations is presented to the reader.

THE NEED FOR A MANAGEMENT SYSTEM

Sophisticated systems of managing production and marketing in industry are the products of an advanced society that has been disciplined by performance standards. Under the pressure of the free-enterprise system and the unremitting demand that large corporations earn profits and pay dividends to stockholders, management efficiency through orientation to results has led to development of management systems such as the one described in this book. Most of the successful corporations in the United States now use annually adopted objectives as a means of

focusing the energies and efforts of managers on the attainment
of goals that are widely known and broadly accepted.

Although the problems of educational management are
obviously quite different from those of the private sector, there
is much to be learned from industry's systems approach in gaining
more efficiency in educational management. The outcomes are
quite similar. As in industry, the leadership in public education
must be dynamic and self-renewing. It must be receptive to feedback that corrects the aim and focus of executives on the school
and college level. A very important practice that will certainly
improve the quality of management in education is for educational institutions, particularly the very large and complex ones,
to become introspectively critical. They must become more introspective about performance if they are to survive and meet
the demands of the future.

The vehicle for attaining performance accountability and
the avenue of assurance that all members of a large and complex
organization, such as a university or city school system, are
striving to reach the same outcomes will be to utilize a management system that assures teamwork and coordination throughout all units of the institution.

The demands upon education are increasing every year.
More is expected of schools and colleges than ever before. The
great social revolution in this country that is insisting that all
citizens regardless of race, ethnic origin, or economic background have an equal opportunity is focusing much of its attention upon our educational establishments. Schools and colleges
must become more performance aware and results oriented.

WHAT MBO WILL DO

School management by objectives focuses on problems.
The management system purports to narrow the gap between
what is and what ought to be. The system demands institutional
introspection. It identifies problems, weaknesses, and inefficien-
cies. It digs out opportunities for high gains at small investment
of time and resources. Problems are systematically identified and
programs are mounted to solve them.

School management by objectives is to the school administrator what a road map and travel itinerary are to an experienced traveler. The administrator knows where he is today. Moreover, he knows how far he has traveled through a series of action steps and performance priorities up to the current date. Then he knows where he is going tomorrow in order to reach an ultimate objective by the time the academic year is concluded. His road maps are the detailed, time-phased action plans developed through the organization's commitment to the management system. From this he has quantitative and qualitative information. Objectivity, system, and order all come from a system of performance accountability.

School management by objectives is to the administrator what a set of football plays and a total game plan are to the athletic coach. The MBO system has a specific assignment for each player on the team. The various players are coordinated and oriented toward the goal. When outcomes are not attained according to plan the top manager knows what has failed and he proceeds to take remedial action to get things back on the track. The analytical aspects of school MBO help the manager to know "what the score is." As in a football game, he operates in a time-phased situation where he knows how much time there is until the end of the game. Not only does each player know his assignment, but he also knows the time phase within which it must be completed if other units are going to be supported as necessary to attain the objectives of the institution by the time the academic year is concluded. MBO provides for both time keeping and score keeping in the educational management game. Moreover, it is not a hit-or-miss proposition with a few rules and many arguments like a sandlot baseball game. There are commitments. There are performance priorities. There are management review sessions. The organization gets where it is going through action-forcing events.

RESULTS-ORIENTED QUESTIONS

The management by objectives system asks questions in terms of results. What are the ultimate consequences of a particular course of action? What are the alternative possibilities in spending money or staff time on one action plan as compared to another? Are there other alternatives? Have we examined the full range of possibilities? Knowing that all problems have a cause, what is the cause of this problem? Was this result too costly? Did we pay more for the educational outcome than it was worth? Even if the educational outcome was worthwhile, could we have gotten more in terms of results by dropping this program and deploying our resources and energies on another? What are we losing in terms of public respect and support and what are we gaining in terms of these same vital outcomes? A well-implemented MBO system in an educational institution asks these hard questions and seeks factual answers.

KEEPING TARGETS BEFORE THE STAFF

School management by objectives helps to keep the staff members from doing what they are not supposed to be doing. The targets are kept up in front of all the members of the team. They are all shooting at the same targets. Moreover, these targets were defined and accepted by the team members before the shooting began. So if some individual isn't doing what the system says that he ought to be doing but is doing something that his special interests or a whim attracts him to be doing, the misperformance will be quickly detected under the management system's procedures. Management by objectives keeps all members of the management team playing the same game because they are reading the same script and concentrating upon goals that have been set through extensive discussion and sharing of ideas. They are also working in priority areas that were determined by consensus.

EDUCATIONAL RESOURCES MANAGEMENT

In addition to the staff, other resources on the campus of an educational organization are coordinated in meeting priorities. The most important problems have prior claim upon the most vital physical facilities. The more short in supply and the greater the demand for facilities of various kinds the more important it is for an educational management system to control their use.

A system of management by objectives obviously must take cognizance of the total resources available. This leads to consideration of facilities, equipment, and supply allocation to support high priority items ahead of less important efforts. This is obviously done by all school administrators with varying degrees of effectiveness. Under a management system that demands performance accountability, action-forcing decisions are made under a system that will not permit delay.

The first principle in economics is that man's resources are limited but his wants are insatiable. School management by objectives helps to deploy resources so that *needs* receive attention ahead of *wants*. Educational institutions will be able to meet more of the genuine needs of education if some of the lesser wants can be systematically eliminated. An effective management system will help educational organizations to take full advantage of its potential by making wise and rational decisions in deploying resources of all kinds. Moreover, resources will be able to meet more of the needs if they are systematically managed to focus upon priority objectives. By so doing, there will be the hope of extending the range of accomplishments so that more priorities can be considered and met.

IMPLICATIONS FOR TRAINING

Many school systems and colleges have extensive inservice training programs. Many of these programs focus upon performance problems without proper analysis. School leaders often resort to extensive training programs to correct a problem that frequently exists because of lack of communication through systematic direction and review to keep staff members working toward solving system-wide problems. Quite often what we think is a gross lack of skill is simply a matter of failure to apply the principles of human behavior in leadership. If staff members are not doing what management expects them to be doing, the chances are that in most cases it is not a training problem.

Educational management by objectives looks at performance deficiencies after having spelled out performance expectations, goals, and action steps. Out of this framework, management is in a much stronger position to analyze the nature of performance deficiencies and to identify genuine (not imaginary) inservice training needs. There is, obviously, a great difference between knowing how to do something and wanting to do it. There is also a great difference between knowing how to do something and not doing it because it is not clearly spelled out as a performance priority for the organization. If a manager wants *actual* performance to be reasonably close to *desired* performance he must analyze the discrepancy between the two. Solutions can often be attained through much simpler and less expensive procedures than launching an extensive training program. School management by objectives helps this analysis to be made and provides the needed information so that solutions can be on target. If lack of skill or knowledge is manifested the specific thrust of the training program can be more adequately defined.

EDUCATIONAL RENEWAL

An educational institution must constantly learn from its operations. Too many programs launched by schools and colleges to solve problems and meet public needs are not subsequently analyzed to see how the efforts hit the targets that were identified when the programs were launched. It is fundamental for individuals, business and corporate institutions, and educational organizations to be growing from what is learned from within as well as from without the confines of the institution. We learn from introspection as well as from instruction and advice from others. School management by objectives tends to keep the institutional mind open.

The life span of productivity and effectiveness of institutions is much like that of individual human beings. Some apparently have a long period of dynamic productivity while others seem to top out and become senile much too early. Of all public institutions, one dedicated to teaching should, itself, assume a stance of teachability. Learning from mistakes, learning from others, reaching and grasping for new ideas that will increase efficiency and improve performance should be a continuous and never-ending process for all schools and colleges.

An open, flexible, problem-solving and alternative-seeking management system will help to keep an educational institution young in spirit and dynamic in performance. Educational renewal is a great problem in the large city school systems and in the huge universities of this nation. Bureaucracies spring up. Personal interests and ambitions color judgments and warp priorities. Renewal and change are extremely difficult in large organizations because of their bureaucratic tendencies.

School management by objectives compels a continuous renewal process to be in motion. An institution cannot operate under a management system of this type without constantly questioning performance, past decisions, and past procedures. The immediate history of the institution is constantly studied as projections are made about new decisions, new plans, and where the next few months will be taking the organization. No institution can operate under such a system without being deeply and continuously involved in badly needed educational renewal processes.

American education has many of the symptoms of rigidity to change and need for renewal. The great universities, for example, change in the face of extraordinary pressure. Departments appear to pursue departmental interests and ignore too often the needs of the total institution and of the students and the general public. This lack of response to the feedback signals calling for change has caused student sit-ins, riots, demonstrations and public refusal to support our institutions at a level commensurate with their needs. The prestige universities of years past are not particularly known for recent, bold, progressive moves. In fact, they are extremely conservative. Their failure to reform and change has been at the root of many recent campus crises.

The great city school systems seem to duplicate the stance of the large universities in conservatism and failure to be responsive to the demands calling for renewal. The size and complexity of these educational organizations make change extremely difficult. These great city school systems need the discipline and stimulation for renewal that come from system-wide application of the principles of MBO. MBO will provide the goal-seeking excitement to generate momentum to solve the great and pressing problems that weigh so heavily upon them.

These problems are, of course, well known to the city school superintendents and university presidents. What is needed is an institution-wide recognition of the problems to be solved and a total management team commitment to specific action steps leading to solutions. As an institution becomes large and complex it also becomes conservative and unresponsive to feedback. A management system, as demonstrated in a number of large corporations, will bring the ends together and place them in the hands of the chief executive so that he can lead and direct and so that he can effectively exhort, encourage, and recognize progress as it is accomplished.

MBO WILL ALSO LEAD TO PERSONAL RENEWAL

Institutional renewal, of course, leads to personal renewal. Like the institution, the staff members must be open and pliable. They must be young in spirit and outlook. The staff must grow in knowledge and technical skill.

Personal renewal comes from constant learning. It comes from both formal and informal teaching. It comes from self-teaching as well as receiving external instruction. It comes from an attitude that knowledge is expanding and that when one stands still he is, in fact, regressing.

Personal renewal comes from a positive attitude toward fair criticism. It comes from being non-defensive and from a desire to be competitive.

To a great extent, age is a state of mind. If is difficult for a person old in years to also become aged in his outlook and attitude if he is constantly learning and growing in competence.

School management by objectives keeps the institutional staff from worrying about the problem of how to keep awake on a full stomach. The management system will teach those who are teachable and keep open of mind and young of spirit those who are seeking renewal.

SUMMARY

All educational organizations need a performance accountability system. The larger the organization the greater the need. An MBO system gives school managers some "power steering" capability that is sorely needed in today's world. This control and responsiveness to need for change will come as the educational institution organizes itself for problem solving.

In the chapters that follow, the MBO system will be described in detail. The steps in an annual management by objectives cycle for schools and colleges will be outlined. Hopefully, the reader will find justification for the author's claim in this chapter that school and college management by objectives will bring about renewal, problem-solving effectiveness, and educational performance accountability.

2

Identifying Educational
Problems Through Needs
Assessment

This chapter discusses the need for a needs assessment program, techniques in involving the staff in needs assessment, the use of tests and other measurements, needs assessments involving sources outside the institution, the use of research capacity, needs assessment questions that should be answered, and the management of a needs assessment program. Additionally, the place of a student and staff personnel profile in needs assessment is described. Two sample summary statements from the needs assessment data-gathering process are provided as further explanation to the reader. The chapter concludes with a discussion of management information systems.

WHY NEEDS ASSESSMENT

As a people, Americans have turned from a preoccupation with production and plenty to a concern for the quality of human life in this nation. We have moved beyond the point where production of the necessities for existence is a concern. We want a rich and meaningful life and we want equality of opportunity for all citizens. The impoverished, the handicapped, and the racial and ethnic minorities in our country are all receiving increasing attention. We have a greater social awareness and a much more sensitive public conscience. Many of the constitutional commitments and assurances to all citizens are at last receiving the attention and concern of government and of the civic leaders of the nation. All of this has led to greater demands upon our schools and institutions of higher learning. Because education is the key to equality of opportunity, education's deficiencies and shortcomings are receiving much more critical attention.

The performance of our schools and colleges is a subject of great concern. More effective teaching of basic skills to low income and minority students, career education, and education for social and citizenship responsibility all represent great demands upon our schools and colleges. Drug abuse, juvenile delinquency, lack of respect for law and order, coping with environmental damage are all problems with which education must be concerned in this new era of social awareness and public concern for the success and happiness of all.

These enormous demands call for systematic attention to the performance outcomes of the schools and colleges of the nation. Since we have so many problems and since our resources are limited, it is essential that we look at the performance of our educational institutions and establish a hierarchy of priorities. We should seek to solve the problems that will do the most in the least time. We should seek to solve the problems that are causing the greatest amount of difficulty and unrest across the nation. We should seek to solve the problems whose solutions will both stimulate the economy and free the public from the burden of supporting citizens who are unable to support themselves. We must, in short, assess our educational needs before establishing our objectives and setting into action leadership and management plans.

The management by objectives system is designed to set priorities based upon needs assessment. Indeed, one of the first steps of the chief executive officer of an educational organization in moving to establish a system of management by objectives is to build a performance profile of his organization. This profile should identify the gaps that exist between what is and what ought to be. Through a comprehensive assessment of needs the school system or university looks at the outputs of the institution.

INVOLVEMENT OF STAFF

It is important to involve the highest possible number of staff members in the needs assessment effort. The first step in solving a problem is, of course, to recognize that the problem exists. The larger the number of persons who recognize and become concerned about the problem, the greater the possibility is that coordinated and comprehensive attention will be focused upon its solution. This is the obvious value of maximum involvement of large numbers of staff members in the needs assessment phase of the management by objectives cycle.

USE OF TESTS IN NEEDS ASSESSMENT

Measurement has always been a problem in education. It is frustrating to admit that we cannot precisely determine how much a student has learned and what value he may ultimately gain from his learning. The real proof of the value of an education comes from observing the life being lived by the individual who was educated. This takes years after formal schooling has ended. These simple facts add to the frustration of assessing accomplishment and identifying performance gaps in our educational system.

As we recognize and emphasize the difficulty in measuring educational performance, we must hasten to add that enormous progress has been made over the past few years in the field of educational tests and measurements. As we admit that we have a long way to go in this area, we must also recognize that we have come a long way.

In looking at the educational attainment of a group of students a number of different sets of relevant data must be correlated. The economic, sociological, psychological, and physical aspects of students must be taken into account as we look at their educational needs and accomplishments. Fortunately, there are a number of attitude and inventory scales that can be used to assess these admittedly difficult-to-measure outcomes.

There are many instruments available for use in measuring various aspects of the educational expectations and actual performance of students. In addition to the well-known measures of academic performance we know much more about measuring ability. What is more, we have normative information on persons of various age groups from all kinds of social and economic backgrounds across the nation. The national assessment of educational progress project sponsored by the Education Commission of the States is but one example of the great new potential of assessing outcomes. Nationally normed tests, inventories and scales of all sorts are also available from reputable publishers.

The standardized measuring instruments have their weaknesses as well as their strengths. All too often, educators concentrate on these weaknesses and use them as excuses for doing little or nothing in needs assessment and in constructing performance profiles that will tell us something about the performance accountability of our schools and colleges. We need a middle ground position between accepting educational tests and measurements as being the final word and denying their use at all because they have some admitted shortcomings.

Through more use of the instruments available we will make progress in developing better instruments. Through more use of these available measures we will also attain more sophistication in how to use them, for what purposes and under what circumstances. School management by objectives demands more use of educational tests and measures. More importantly, specific action is planned as an outcome of the tests and measurements program.

All too often, testing programs are administered in education only to have the results put on the shelf and ignored by teachers and administrators. School MBO programs generate results awareness. Standardized test information becomes part of the active information used in the daily operations of the institution.

Standardized tests should be used, of course, to improve

instruction. Test results can be helpful both in defining goals and in identifying gaps in learning performance. Tests can help educators to understand the student's development at a particular time in his educational career. They can also help tell about his potential for the future. Tests can reveal difficulties and help educators to do curriculum planning and make decisions on instructional improvement.

Standardized educational tests and measures can, of course, be misused. There can be harmful aspects of tests such as too much reliance upon them and their use for purposes for which they were not developed. Rarely is it possible to take the results of one test and arrive at a precise decision concerning what to do or what to recommend for a student. Usually a number of factors must be weighed in such decision making.

In a needs assessment program under an MBO effort the tests of many students are examined. Even in these circumstances multiple factors must be weighed in providing information that will permit the administrator to assess performance priorities and allocate resources. The comparative information from standardized tests will permit an educational institutional to arrive at certain reasonably valid conclusions about the performance of the institution as compared to others of similar circumstances with students of approximately the same characteristics and background. Improved practices in establishing national norms have made the task of assessment much less difficult.

An important side benefit from utilizing test data in an MBO system is that misinformation and misuse come under closer scrutiny. Henry Chauncey and John E. Dobbin,* in their very informative book on testing, claim that a certain amount of "misinformed folklore" has grown up around testing practices in colleges and school systems. These distinguished authors believe that tests are tools of teaching that will be useful only if they help the teacher perform more effectively. They claim that one test a

---

*Henry Chauncey and John E. Dobbin, *Testing: Its Place in Education Today* (Harper & Row, New York, 1963), p. 68.

year can be too much if the results are not fully utilized. But, these authors say, where a testing program has been made an integral part of teaching and where the results of testing are constantly utilized to identify weak spots in educational institutions the results can be very worthwhile in making the teaching and learning performance of a total institution more results oriented.

The use of standardized tests on both the college and the school level is widespread at the present time. It is safe to say that it would be difficult to find a college or public school system that does not have some sort of standardized testing program. Individual teachers and perhaps separate school units in a public school system or a separate department on a university campus may be utilizing test results for educational decision making.

What is needed is an institution-wide or school system-wide assessment of educational needs with the standardized testing program playing a key role in providing one important component of information on the quest for improved performance. Each year millions of students are affected by decisions made by administrators. Billions of dollars are spent in educational programs. By becoming more results oriented through institution-wide needs assessment efforts we will be able to spend our dollars and personnel resources more wisely in reaching the educational objectives of our schools and colleges.

From the standardized testing program, vital needs assessment information about the learning ability of students, how well students can use the basic tools of academic learning, and many other important aspects of needs identification will be attained.

Tests have been used to give specific information about individual students. They should, of course, continue to be used for that purpose. But in an MBO needs assessment program tests can also tell an institution how well it is doing and what results its current priorities are gaining. Tests can be instructive to the college department as a whole. They can be important links in the total chain of information that a large and complex institution such as a school district or university can use to forge new programs of action that will be responsive to the real needs of the clientele served by the institution.

NEEDS ASSESSMENT FROM SOURCES
OUTSIDE THE INSTITUTION

Parents, employers, alumni, and other governmental agencies are important sources of needs assessment information. Schools and colleges, if they are to be introspective about performance results, should deliberately assess the viewpoints of individuals, organizations, and institutions outside of the educational establishment. Obviously, such assessments must take into account the source of the information.

It is important, for example, for a public school to know how parents view the school. Simple surveys and questionnaires provide essential feedback even if many opinions are unfair and based upon misinformation. The fact that significant numbers of parents have such opinions is vital information for school managers. Too many schools move along in almost total ignorance insofar as seeing things as others see them is concerned.

On the college level the important information about the performance of the institution contained in the combined wisdom of thousands of graduates is often largely ignored. In a needs assessment program, surveys of persons having had an opportunity to reflect upon the value of college studies should be utilized for the great potential that exists for decision-making and priority-setting purposes.

The Utah State Department of Education conducted a needs project to identify the most critical educational needs in the public schools of Utah. The reader is referred to Appendix A for a detailed report of a comprehensive needs assessment project.

USE OF RESEARCH CAPACITY

The information-gathering capacity of colleges and universities is well known. The great research potential of our universities has been developed by application of the scientific method to problem-solving tasks. Man's discovery of new knowledge has been greatly accelerated by the quest for truth that has been led by our universities. It is lamentable that our universities have not turned this fact-finding and information-gathering capacity upon the institutions themselves. There needs to be more concern for the teaching and learning process on the college campus. The research talent of the college and university should be directed more inwardly so that needs for improvement can be identified and promising practices can be developed. Colleges need to know much more about teaching and learning performance on the campus.

Since the graduates are more mature, constructive criticism and suggestions for improvement will be much more useful to colleges than similar feedback efforts to graduates of public schools. This research- and information-gathering potential becomes a ready resource in a needs assessment program on the college campus. This applies not only to gaining survey-type information from the graduates, but also to many other aspects in the total needs assessment program.

Colleges can use needs assessment information in fund raising and in working with legislative bodies to defend appropriations requests. By being better informed about past performance, outstanding accomplishments can be identified and provided to influential sources for the benefit of the institution. This important product of assessing needs through the university's conducting a comprehensive study of itself will justify the effort.

NEEDS ASSESSMENT QUESTIONS

In seeking information concerning educational needs, individuals and organizations outside the institution should be asked to respond to inquiries that will lead to some definitive answers to the following questions:

1. What should be the priority goals of the institution?
2. What are the performance deficiencies of the institution?
3. What is the institution doing that it should not do and what is the institution not doing that it should be doing?
4. What desired competencies in the students should receive more emphasis and what deficiencies should be given more attention?

5. What should be done to improve the reputation and image of the institution?
6. Is the economy of the community being effectively enhanced by the efforts of the institution?
7. What past practices of the institution have caused people to be "up tight?"
8. Is the institution sufficiently warm and humane in responding to the people who come to it for assistance and services?
9. Are there problems in reaching persons in the institution and in expressing views and getting answers to questions?
10. Taking into account the fact that the resources and the amount of money available are limited, what programs in the institution should be given more emphasis and what should be given less?

The foregoing suggested questions are quite broad and general. In developing a survey instrument to gain information, a much more definitive and detailed questionnaire would need to be developed. The broad questions outlined above could be utilized as a guide in formulating a more detailed survey instrument to gain the information needed in the needs assessment program.

Usually, a needs assessment effort provides open-ended questions so that any specific item that may have been overlooked can be responded to by the person or organization to whom the inquiry is being directed.

MANAGING THE NEEDS ASSESSMENT PROGRAM

The needs assessment program should involve a broad and representative sample of personnel of the entire institution or school system. The actual work of the needs assessment program must, however, be directed from one office. The responsibility should be fixed and the work to be done must be clearly understood and carefully outlined. Both schools and colleges have conducted accreditation surveys where the attention of the institution is focused upon itself. This experience and expertise should be utilized in the needs assessment program. Needs assessment and accreditation information surveys are quite similar activities and some of the same personnel might well be used in assessing needs.

In conducting a comprehensive needs assessment the assessors must keep before them the statements of purposes, roles, and other broad policy commitments that have been made by the governing boards and the people that support the institution. This will provide a reasonably explicit definition of the reason for the existence of the institution.

Additionally, the broader goals of the community served by the institution and wider definitions of purposes of other important segments of the society should be kept in mind. Then, as the needs assessment program moves forward, questions can be directed form this background knowledge with full confidence that there are some fairly well-accepted broad and general outcomes that the institution should be seeking. The needs assessment program and the subsequent statement of performance priorities by the chief executive will help the institution to get down to these crucial decisions.

ACTION PLANS

The managers of the needs assessment program should develop an action plan with certain responsibilities explicitly stated and accomplishment deadlines set. These managers can then monitor the progress of the institution-wide assessment effort. This will include such things as providing forms, developing computer programs, making contacts with key persons both inside and outside the institution. It will also include the mobilization of the talent needed for the brief time required to complete the needs assessment. Those who administer the needs assessment program have a special responsibility to offer the kinds of reassurances that are necessary to all concerned.

The needs assessment program must not become a witch hunt. It must be made clear at the outset that the institution as a whole is seeking information that will result in institution-wide improvement. The purpose of needs assessment is not one of blame fixing or faultfinding. As good as the institution might be the attitude should be that decisions have to be made and priorities set. This cannot be done without a broad information base. The needs assessment program is the effort to gain the information that will identify needs and place all such needs before decision makers so that the most important ones get attention ahead of the least important ones. All of this is, of course, so easy to say that it may seem trite. It is important, however, that the total school system or entire university receive assurance that the needs assessment program is seeking facts upon which future decisions can be made.

In conducting the needs assessment program, those responsible for managing it must keep in mind that the means of gathering information should not become so involved that they become ends. Ends and means are often confused with the result that too much emphasis is put on the means and they then become the ends. The needs assessment effort is not the problem-solving effort. It merely identifies the problems by shedding further light and making a searching analysis possible. If, in the needs assessment program, we are able to get most of the facts and find out precisely where we are, we will be able to take the results as baseline data. We are then in a position to outline parameters within which we will be operating. This is essential before we begin to plan for changes and to marshal efforts that will result in a redirection of our resources.

Another caution for the managers of the needs assessment program is that they must avoid such a comprehensive and detailed effort that the costs and time commitments are excessive. The entire effort should be compressed into a few brief weeks and emphasis should be on utilization of existing data where such is available. Needless to say, the institution must move on. It has certain calendar commitments it is expected to meet. The needs assessment program must do the best that can be done within the realistic time frames that are placed upon it. Needs assessment is a continuous process and the managers must keep in mind that if they wait for the ultimate in all data they are certainly going to get bogged down.

In this regard, it is useful to recall the deliberations of Benjamin Franklin when he was establishing his first academy He was reported to have remarked quite sadly that it would be well if his students could be taught all things that were useful and also all things that were artistic and ornamental in nature. In comtemplating this, he opined that both time and resources were short and that he would therefore have to assess with some degree of assurance those things that were the *most* useful and those things that were the *most* ornamental. Out of this information he would then set his priorities.

This is the circumstance in which the chief executive officer finds himself. The needs assessors will help by providing the kind of information that will shed light upon determining which efforts will be of the most worth and which ones appear to be of the least value.

THE STUDENT AND STAFF PERSONNEL PROFILE

A departmental or school student and staff personnel profile, constructed from needs assessment information, will provide information in greater depth than is typically found in most school or college operations. The characteristics of the student populations being served and the social, economic, racial, and ethnic make-up of the community or neighborhood must be weighed in making assumptions on performance expectations. An objective, expressed in anticipated performance results, must take into account the characteristics of the students, the neighborhood and community.

Since needs assessment will help provide information to set objectives, the following information about the clientele served by the educational institution will be important in interpreting the significance of educational achievement, dropout rate data, school attendance, problems of disruptive and emotionally disturbed students:

1. Racial and ethnic mix of the student and community population.

2. Student transiency (high or low rate of move-ins and move-outs).
3. Number of families on welfare, number of children on AFDC (federally supported aid to families of dependent children).
4. Income level of workers, professionals and self-employed residents.
5. Number of single parent (divorced, widow, etc.) heads of families.
6. Information from law enforcement agencies and the courts on the amount of crime and delinquency in the neighborhood.

All of the foregoing information will be relevant if placed in a comparative context. School systems, college student bodies, school unit neighborhoods, and college departmental student clientele can then be compared with others of similar characteristics. A school with 87% attendance and a dropout rate double that of other school attendance areas may be performing at a high level when the information outlined above is taken into consideration. This comparative context will be very important in establishing performance expectations.

The profile should also look at professional personnel and other employees who work for the school or department. Is the faculty new and inexperienced? Is it heavily staffed with older teachers lacking in recency of training? What about teacher turnover, absenteeism, and sick leave records?

Enrollments in some departments of instruction in colleges and secondary schools may have a relationship to characteristics of the faculty. Dropout rates and changes in course registration may be related to faculty make-up. An increase in dropout rates in some schools may correlate closely with changes taking place in the make-up of the neighborhood.

A certain number of baseless assumptions exist in school systems and on university campuses because information akin to that identified above is not systematically compiled and analyzed. School units assumed to be heavily impacted with problems related to the make-up of the neighborhood may be far from what was assumed. More mythology than fact stands behind many management decisions that are made because of neglect of this vital information-gathering and data-analysis task.

If we are to make valid conclusions about performance expectations, and if we are to make management decisions about performance priorities, we must have information in depth about the factors that impact upon a student body.

SUMMARY STATEMENTS FROM NEEDS ASSESSMENT DATA

The purpose of needs assessment is best illustrated by presenting some sample summary statements that point out problems and suggest priorities. The following examples will help the reader to see the significance of the needs assessment effort:

1. From the Canyon Rim Elementary School of the Granite School District:

The average daily attendance at the Canyon Rim School dropped to its lowest level of 95% of enrollment during the past year. The following indicates this steady attendance decline:

1965-66	95.7%
1966-67	96.3%
1967-68	96.4%
1968-69	95.3%
1969-70	95.6%
1970-71	95.0%

2. From the Bureau of Education for the Handicapped, U.S. Office of Education:

There are 7 million school-age handicapped children (age 5-18 years) in the U.S. who require special educational assistance. Only 40% of them are receiving such services. There are 125,000 teachers of the handicapped, about half of whom are estimated to be uncertified and need further training. Of the 40% of the total handicapped children receiving special instruction, half that number are being taught by inadequately trained teachers.

The above are samples of products from needs assessment that can be used by management to look at gaps in performance and weigh comparative needs for deployment of resources. As the chief executive officer gets ready to announce performance priorities (as discussed in the following chapter), a number of summary statements such as these will give him an opportunity to look at the total universe of educational needs and deficiencies.

MANAGEMENT INFORMATION SYSTEMS
AND NEEDS ASSESSMENT

The entire thrust of the needs assessment effort is to gather information critical to setting priorities and making management decisions. A number of school systems and a lesser number of colleges and universities are moving toward establishing a system for gathering, validating, and interpreting information crucial to management of education. Most of these efforts try to center in one place an information center that receives reports and makes available to all members of the management team various types of information useful to managers. A small staff is established under the direction of a person who coordinates the gathering, processing and dissemination of management information. Copies of all reports and other paper work that contain information pertinent to management decision making are typically forwarded to the management information center.

By keeping the management information system current and by making sure that the data are carefully interpreted and accurately stated, the management information staff provides a vital service to decision makers.

In a large educational organization a network of management information contributors work part time under a management system coordinator to provide information from the various departments and units of the institution. In a large school district, for example, one secretary in each school unit is typically assigned the responsibility of writing certain items of information needed in the management information system. Experience has shown that this requires only two or three hours of work each month. A full-time secretary in each unit is not necessary to make the network functional.

The management information system coordinator usually calls meetings at periodic intervals to give instructions to the contributors from the different school units or departments of the institution. At these meetings problems are identified and instructions are clarified. Suggestions are received to improve the system. The elimination of redundant information in the system can receive constant attention from those involved in making it work.

Some items of information in a management information system must be kept current on a monthly basis while other items may only require updating once a year. Usually the contributors to the system have a schedule established by the person who coordinates the program so that they know when certain sheets that make up the total management information book are due. This procedure of updating keeps the top leadership operating with a system of current information. As they assess needs and set priorities that are essential to a good program of performance accountability, the information system helps them act under the assurance that they are not making decisions from stale information.

The administrators who have management information books (usually in loose-leaf form) on their desks have a responsibility to help keep the management information system related to what is actually needed to make decisions. Most coordinators of a management information system have learned that it is useful to know how frequently an item of information is referred to and used by a manager. He therefore provides a check-off box on each sheet of information. When a manager refers to a certain item of information he can quickly make a check mark with his pen. Then when the management information staff removes a page to put a current item in its place they can refer to the number of check marks and know immediately that the page of information has had heavy use, moderate use, very little use, or no use at all since the last time the item was placed in the management information book. This, quite obviously, helps the operators of the system make decisions on removing or keeping certain items in the book. A similar feedback method from the managers using the information system is necessary to learn if information is sufficiently complete or if additional data or different treatment of the data would serve management more effectively.

In large educational organizations it is common for the public to become confused with conflicting statistics released by various parts and pieces of the college or school bureaucracy. If all managers who give answers and provide information to the public are referring to the same basic source book this confusion and conflict can largely be eliminated. The management information system also serves, in this capacity, as a vital public information source and as a means of establishing constituency confidence from outside the organization.

Another common practice in the operation of management information systems is to require a date and a signature from the person in the organization responsible for providing the information. If, for example, a school attendance report is required monthly, the secretary who functions as a contributor prepares the report to be submitted to the information system and the principal signs and dates it. This fixes responsibility for the information and makes it possible to go back to the original source if some controversy arises over its accuracy.

In a system of school management by objectives this technique of gaining performance accountability in submitting information is essential. It is, however, more important to the person submitting the information since he is able to certify that that was the statistical situation at the time that he submitted it. The signing and dating of the report provides him with the kind of security and definitiveness that he deserves to have. Likewise, the top managers in the organization can qualify any information that they provide after they have looked at the management information sheet and have taken into consideration the fact that a certain amount of time has elapsed since the information was submitted.

In a needs assessment program conducted as one of the important steps in setting objectives and establishing performance accountability in an educational organization, a management information system like the one described is very useful and almost essential. A central management information clearinghouse makes it easy for administrators to monitor progress in reaching objectives. The entire needs assessment program, if it is centered in the MIS office, is conducted with less difficulty and with more reliability.

It is the opinion of the author that some type of supervised management information system is necessary in modern school and college administration. Such a system takes on even more importance if the educational institution is operating under a management by objectives program.

SUMMARY

The need for a needs assessment program and the value of extensive involvement of the staff have been emphasized in this chapter. Needs assessment as a status study through use of test data, student and staff information profiles has been described. The management of the needs assessment program must avoid the trap of extensive paper work and too much detail. Currently available data from standardized testing programs and from accreditation surveys should keep the task within bounds.

A management information system should eventually emerge from needs assessment and the total MBO effort. This system will help the management team in decision making and will make future needs assessment efforts more simple to execute at less cost in staff time and money.

3

The Chief Executive's Performance Priorities

In this chapter the identification and function of the chief executive's performance priorities will be discussed. Some sample performance priority statements will be presented to the reader. The need for system-wide discussion of performance priorities by the staff prior to final adoption by the chief executive will be emphasized.

FUNCTION OF PERFORMANCE PRIORITIES IN A RESULTS-ORIENTED EDUCATIONAL ORGANIZATION

After the school system or university has completed its needs assessment the staff is ready to present the data indicating the most critical educational needs to the organization's chief executive officer. From this assessment the chief executive will identify his goals and set out in some detail the key problems of the organization. These problems will usually be those that can be solved with minimal effort and cost of time as related to effectiveness. They are, however, high priority needs that demand solution if the organization is to move ahead in fulfilling its mission during the coming academic year. These needs and problems to be solved are identified in the management by objectives system as *performance priorities.*

Performance priorities tell the administrative team members where the school system or college is going and where it wants to be in terms of *performance outcomes* at the conclusion of the coming academic year. Through announcing his performance priorities, the chief executive calls for discussion and response that should lead to consensus and action throughout the entire organization. The management by objectives system brings this about, and the top leader in the organization leads through his performance priorities. This chapter describes how this is done under the democratic concept of participative management.

This chapter will: (1) present two sample performance priority descriptions, (2) discuss system-wide goals and how they relate to school unit or college department objectives, (3) point out how some performance priorities become a major objective in one unit of the organization and an objective of lesser importance in other units, (4) describe how performance priorities trigger feedback and system-wide dialogue on the total problems of the organization, and (5) explain how performance priorities challenge units into a system-wide response that commits action on critical problems.

TWO EXAMPLES OF PERFORMANCE PRIORITY DESCRIPTIONS

Two persistent problems in education that are common to most educational organizations in the nation are identified below as sample performance priority descriptions. One comes from the management by objectives system of the U.S. Office of Education and the other from the MBO program of Utah's largest school system:

Performance Priority Statement on Education of the Handicapped Issued by the U. S. Commissioner of Education

There are an estimated seven million school age handicapped children in the United States who require some special educational assistance. Only 40% of them are receiving such services. The lack of proper special education programs in local school districts is caused by the much higher cost of educating handicapped children, the small numbers of qualified teachers, inadequate earmarked resources, and an uneven national commitment to education of the handicapped.

Effective educational practices developed by one school or by one institution are not systematically disseminated and adopted by others. A number of such programs are known to exist and a method must be developed to assure their widespread adoption.

Through proper special education many handicapped persons can learn to become self-sufficient at least to the degree of not requiring institutional services for years. It has been estimated that it costs approximately $250,000 for a state to support one mental retardate for life.

We are increasingly aware of a need to provide career education for every handicapped child. Research findings indicate that the pre-school education of handicapped children will reduce expenses of special education as the handicapped child grows older.

A national commitment to this proposed goal and to the development of resources necessary to meet that commitment is essential.

This performance priority statement by the U. S. Commissioner of Education calls attention to an urgent national problem in education. Moreover, it states briefly that evidence is available to substantiate the need. It mentions some aspects of the priority that should gain the attention of several of the Bureaus of the U. S. Office of Education.

The Commissioner does not demand specific reaction from the Bureaus. He points out the potential for response and waits for his key managers in the organization to react to his performance priority. This allows the action to grow from within the organization, and the goals become *agency-wide action priorities rather than Commissioner's goals imposed from the top.*

Performance Priority Statement on
Student Attendance Issued by the
Superintendent of the Granite School
District (Salt Lake County, Utah)

One of the first indicators of failure in school is poor attendance. Studies of dropouts and of students in trouble almost always show a high correlation with poor attendance. School attendance percentages have been declining in recent years on a nation-wide scale. Some observers consider this phenomenon to be part of the alienation of students from school and from society in general.

Poor school attendance leads to discouragement as the student faces make-up work and copes with a host of personal problems related to a break in the continuity of the school program. Poor attendance causes extra work for heavily burdened teachers as they struggle with problem students who have missed important instruction in the classroom sessions planned for all.

In the Granite School District we have a total enrollment of over 63,000 students. Our average daily attendance, however, is only 58,000. Approximately 5,000 students are absent from school each day. This represents a loss educationally that is hard to comprehend. Additionally, it represents a huge dollar loss for the district and for each school in the system. It represents a loss in dollars for teaching supplies and teacher salaries. For every 27 students in Utah in average daily attendance the state aid formula guarantees $11,600. From these data it is easy to calculate the financial loss we are suffering from steadily declining school attendance.

Some schools in the district, serving minority and low income families, have a great challenge to look at school attendance as a performance improvement priority. Every school in the Granite system should consider the improvement of school attendance as a matter for discussion and possible action.

This performance priority statement gives specific data to substantiate the problem. The statement appeals to the educators' interest in problem students. It points out the added burden on busy teachers. It indicates the financial implications of poor attendance. The statement is written to appeal to the many interests of a large school system and the diverse population of a metropolitan area where attendance varies greatly.

In Appendix C will be found some performance priority statements issued by the Superintendent of the Granite School District, Salt Lake City, Utah. The reader will note that some priorities quote specific data to note deficiencies while others merely give explanatory and descriptive statements. In either case, however, problems must be described in quantifiable terms as they become specific operational objectives (as discussed in Chapter 4).

SYSTEM-WIDE GOALS AND SCHOOL UNIT OR COLLEGE DEPARTMENT OBJECTIVES

Like the two sample performance priority descriptions presented above, many educational problems defy solution from year to year because of failure to focus attention of the entire institution or total school system upon them. Education does not become more effective merely through the identification of problems. Our educational organizations must be managed to systematically solve the problems that we have known to be high priority concerns for a long time. The chief executive officer's performance priority statements are the first step in a crusade to become more efficient and to practice educational renewal through use of a management system that solves problems and renews the effectiveness of the educational units.

The performance priorities submitted to the department heads or school principals become the topics around which much dialogue must flow prior to school unit or departmental action of formal adoption of objectives (as discussed in Chapter 4) for the coming academic year. The dialogue is most essential in an MBO system. The principles of democracy and participative management demand this essential discussion and response.

The chief executive of the organization does not directly set or impost the objectives for the school principals or college department heads. By sending out his performance priority statements that were derived from a needs assessment in which the staff members were involved, he is, in effect, telling each administrator to consider the priorities as a statement of system-wide or campus-wide problems *as he sees them*. He is asking each unit to consider them, to discuss and react to them, and to weigh them carefully in setting objectives for the coming academic year. He is calling attention to problems, and he is implying that each unit should consider weaving into the fabric of its total operational plan some of the thread of the institution-wide performance concerns.

The publication of performance priorities must be followed by central office staff discussion of the entire rationale for the priorities and their significance to each particular unit. This must be done in a manner that calls for response, for rebuttal, and for change and improvement before final adoption for action. The discussion with central office staff must be in the form of a soft sell and mild defense of the tentative list of concerns. It must generate awareness of the problems and stimulate concern for solution.

The performance priorities are not a casual list to be taken lightly, however. They must be defensible before being promulgated, and they should be substantive enough to lead to a possible identification of final action targets. They must ultimately lead to objectives and sub-objectives in the units of the organization and they must commit action to problems and their solution if they are ultimately adopted as objectives following staff debate and discussion.

In Appendix C will be found five performance priority descriptions, the first of which is the performance priority on school attendance. The reader will note that this description calls attention to a steadily declining situation. The priority is defensible; it is sufficiently substantive as a system-wide priority since the declining condition is found in many schools. This priority can easily lead to objectives and sub-objectives in the units of the organization. The priority should commit action to problem solving if it is accepted as a major objective.

The other sample performance priority descriptions in Appendix C should also lead to performance commitments described in the previous paragraph. These examples are all broad enough to have system-wide appeal and to leave room for local initiatives.

The chief executive wisely permits the action response to emerge from within each administrative unit. The objectives and time-phased action steps that follow must emerge from *within* the organization and not be imposed downward from the top. Thus, the performance priorities set the framework and point the direction. The specific objectives that grow from the priorities are more definitive and more action oriented than the performance priorities. (A more detailed discussion of this follows in the next chapter.)

SCHOOL UNIT OR COLLEGE DEPARTMENT EMPHASIS ON DIFFERENT PERFORMANCE PRIORITIES

The performance priorities will have varied implications for different units in the school system or college. An instructional goal will be of prime concern, obviously, to instructional units. An instructional need will call for supportive action from other units or departments such as finance and student personnel services. Conversely, a priority to improve financial management information will be a major concern for the business office, and it will usually require supportive action from almost every unit in the organization.

An effective management by objectives system must coordinate the points of major leadership responsibility and the points of required supportive action from one unit to another. Therefore, all performance priorities should be discussed by all units. The interest and intensity of discussion will vary.

As performance priorities are identified from the chief executive's office, suggested prime and supporting roles will necessarily emerge before action responsibility is fixed. Experienced leaders usually encourage reaching out initiatives for support from within the organization. This activity creates a side benefit from MBO. An awareness of need for reciprocal assistance to meet objectives leads to teamwork and harmony in the system. Experience indicates that multi-unit committees emerge and membership in managing affairs from one department to another breaks down some of the walls that have existed for a long time prior to MBO. Avenues to communication and genuine understanding across academic departments are born out of necessity. Institutional rivalries become less sharp when reciprocal favors are asked and granted. It usually becomes necessary for the central office to offer coordination in cross-unit planning but the responsibility for gaining cross-unit support is most often left in the shop of the unit with the major responsibility for the performance priority.

If, for example, a performance priority on a college campus calls for a new effort in standardized testing and measurement of certain outcomes and competencies in the student body of the institution, the major load would obviously rest with the student personnel and psychological testing department. The Director and his staff would need extensive support from academic departments throughout the campus. The initiative should rest with the Director and his staff to gain this support with the front office helping and encouraging the cooperation. This follows the philosophy of permitting and encouraging maximum initiative for problem solving to flow from within the organization without imposition from above. Contrary to some views, MBO encourages this type of action and leads to a decrease in the academic feudal system's self-interest needs becoming foremost in resource commitment. This desired outcome will be especially evident where performance priority discussion is discouraged in an atmosphere around the campus or school system where staff dare to challenge the chief executive and add and subtract from his views before final action plans are committed.

The management by objectives system will be authoritarian if the chief executive's leadership personality makes it that way. It is, however, a management system that lends itself most easily to democratic procedures of participative management. This becomes quite evident as the units of the organization discuss the performance priorities and trade commitments of support across departmental or school unit boundaries.

BENEFITS FROM SYSTEM-WIDE DISCUSSION OF THE CHIEF EXECUTIVE'S PERFORMANCE PRIORITIES

One of the biggest dividends from a management by objectives system of leadership comes to the entire campus or school system from the necessity for extensive conversation — openly and freely engaged in at all levels — about the gaps that exist between what is and what ought to be in the entire institution. This most profound discussion must follow the publication of the performance priorities and it must precede adoption of specific objectives.

Interested professionals think through at least once each year what their priorities should be and on what outcomes the total organization should be working during the coming academic year. The chief executive's annual list of performance priorities tosses out to the total staff a challenge to agree and support the priorities or present alternatives that are more worthy of high priority concern and action.

The chief executive — if he is open and mature in his leadership — will welcome this system-wide response. He will know that he takes his stand and commits himself to leadership initiative through his performance priorities. He will also know that the open attitude of seeking debate and candid response will lead to an improved focus of the institution on the goals for the coming academic year.

The attitude of the chief executive is a vital key to the entire MBO system. It is expressed more in how he advances his performance priorities into specific objectives for each operating unit than in any other aspect of MBO activity. He must have a dynamic leadership style that provokes and encourages system-wide renewal effort through constantly managing to reach greater heights. His leadership personality must manifest itself first in how it genuinely seeks feedback and debate.

The whole purpose of the dialogue on his priorities is to gain unity in the system. If skillfully directed, the response to his priorities will lead to a clearly defined sense of direction for the college or school system. The importance of the priorities having sufficient depth and meaning to unify cannot be overemphasized.

SUMMARY

Performance priorities provide a unique opportunity for the chief executive to identify to the entire organization the problems that should be solved during the coming academic year. By publishing his priorities and calling for debate, discussion, and response, he is executing his leadership responsibility to take a stand on issues. He is expressing his desire that all staff members participate fully before objectives and action steps are committed.

The two sample performance priority statements in this chapter cite specific data from needs assessment work to substantiate the concern that the chief executive expressed for more attention to problems identified. Both examples called for response from a number of units in the organizations involved. They were broadly based priorities that would provoke discussion and response. They called for action but did not impose any specific demand.

Action on priorities should come from within the organization and not be imposed from the top down. It should emerge from discussion and recognition of the gaps that exist between what is and what should be in the organization.

Performance priorities should focus on attainable goals and problems that can be solved with minimal effort and resources.

Some priorities are of only minimal concern to some units and a major burden for others. Most priorities will call for cooperation across unit boundaries and will result in improved communication and understanding.

Management by objectives can be the door to a truly democratic, open system of leadership if the chief executive's leadership style of operation and personality will encourage the same. The performance priorities should gain the benefits of participative management and should unify the system around a clear definition of goals and objectives.

After the performance priorities have been adopted in final form, the school units or college departments are ready to establish operational objectives that will be responsive to the priorities.

4

Establishing Operational Objectives

This chapter describes how the performance priorities are converted into the operational objectives that become accomplishment commitments for the academic year. How to write objectives in quantifiable and time-sequenced terms will be described. Reasons for limiting the total number of objectives and the need for extensive staff participation will be explained in the pages that follow.

OPERATIONAL PLANNING

After the processes outlined in Chapters 2 and 3 have been completed, the school system or university is ready to do its operational planning for the coming academic year. Each major unit in the educational organization will have received the revised performance priorities from the chief executive. These priorities will be examined carefully to determine implications they might have for action on the part of each unit.

As a response to his performance priorities the chief executive will request from each department statements of objectives that will contribute to solutions of the problems identified through the needs assessment effort. Through these objectives the results to be achieved by the school or department are predetermined as accurately as possible. Every objective will constitute a commitment to attain some very definite performance outcomes by the end of the academic year.

Insofar as operational planning is concerned an objective is an organizational pledge to make a special effort to attain a highly desirable result. These objectives are committed to writing. They constitute a performance commitment. This commitment should be stated clearly enough so that it can be easily determined when it has been reached.

NEED FOR STAFF PARTICIPATION

In keeping with the central idea of involving most of the staff in the needs assessment process and in the dialogue and critique leading up to the final revisions of the chief executive's performance priorities, this democratic procedure of participatory decision making in establishing the specific operational objectives of the school or department should be followed. School teachers and college professors deserve and will demand the opportunity to help set the performance standards against which their organization will strive to measure itself during the coming academic year. Those largely responsible for accomplishing the objectives need to have a major voice in helping to determine the level of attainment and the specific results to which the unit will pre-commit itself. Ideally, through this process of involvement each individual staff member will know and understand what level of attainment is considered successful since he will have had an opportunity to define success. The personal involvement and commitment will help the professional members of the school or college department to answer questions such as: (1) What results are expected of me? (2) Am I performing effectively in contributing to the standards of performance for the unit? (3) In personal terms, what level of performance is considered successful?

The specific objectives to be attained during the academic year will lead to the desired teamwork that MBO should accomplish if the individual staff members are seriously addressing themselves to these three questions. The personal goals and commitments that grow out of participation in setting the objectives for the coming academic year will lead to the desired results-oriented effort that MBO strives to attain.

HOW TO WRITE OBJECTIVES

Objectives should be written using quantitative language. The anticipated results should be stated in numbers, percentages, ratios, or in some other very definite measurable terms. When the objective has been written in such a manner that the result can be measured and is countable to such an extent that the success level is well understood by the entire staff, it will be sufficiently specific. (In Appendix B will be found some sample objectives that meet these criteria. Note that they contain quantitative language, that anticipated results are described in measurable terms.)

Contributors to the accomplishment of the objective will be able to regularly experience a sense of progress, momentum, and accomplishment. Clarity and ease in evaluation must guide the writing of the operational objectives of each department or school unit in the educational institution.

TWO QUESTIONS ANSWERED

Operational objectives should answer these two questions: (1) What is it we must accomplish? (2) How will we know when we have accomplished it? These are obviously quite simple questions, but they are difficult to answer in simple, concise, and quantifiable language. Very few educational systems operate under the performance accountability discipline implied by these simple questions. That is why the writing of performance objectives in the manner advocated in this chapter is important to school managers interested in results-oriented operations.

In a subsequent chapter we will discuss the selection of the most efficient means of arriving at the destinations described in the operational objectives. This chapter is limited to a discussion of stating objectives clearly and unequivocally and in a manner that will make it possible for administrators and staff to know when they have attained their objectives.

THE CHARACTERISTICS OF A CLEARLY STATED OBJECTIVE

A discussion of the characteristics of a well-written objective should help to communicate more about how to write objectives and how the writing of them will help educational leaders become better managers. Keeping in mind that objectives should state some intended outcomes, the staff should write objectives to maximize the probability of achieving these outcomes.

Be sure to communicate performance *intent.* Objectives in an educational institution should be written by an individual or committee after a great amount of input has been gained from the staff members who will be responsible for accomplishing them. In this regard, it is good practice to state an objective as concisely as possible and then get an interpretation of the performance intent from colleagues. When the staff members have given a written objective to others who then can clearly explain how they will know that they have attained the end result specified in the objective, they will know that they have written a clear, concise and unambiguous objective. From this they have a valuable management tool to use for the coming academic year. If, on the other hand, in a discussion with colleagues the operational planners find that the intent was not interpreted as it was written it will be obvious that they will have problems all year in managing the organization to attain that particular objective. Further, when in a discussion with colleagues it is indicated that they had something else in mind or that something more or something less than was intended has been implied from reading the objective, it will be known that more concise and descriptive language is needed.

All elements of ambiguity must be eliminated. In short, the staff will know that there will be debate and discussion and possible contention throughout the entire year if the written statement of a major objective does not do a good job of communicating a specific performance intent to which the organization is about to commit itself for the academic year.

Generally speaking, writers of performance objectives should avoid words that have several meanings or to which there can be many interpretations. Loaded words and words that cannot be interpreted in terms of performance results will lead to difficulty. It should be remembered that a major objective is a statement of performance intent to which an entire school or college department plans to commit itself for a full academic year. The statement of the objective must communicate in a way that will preclude misinterpretation.

WRITING HARD-TO-DEFINE OBJECTIVES

There are many highly desirable educational outcomes that schools and colleges ought to attain that are difficult to quantify. For example, consider an objective in which students should be taught to appreciate something or to understand, enjoy, or believe something. Considerable descriptive language needs to be built around the somewhat ambiguous words that can be subjected to numerous interpretations. It does not necessarily follow that we should totally avoid such terms as "appreciate" or "enjoy." But if these words are used, considerable effort should be spent in explaining what is meant by writing as many specific statements as might be necessary to make sure that the intent is communicated and that the result can be quantified as much as possible. This is done by specifying outcomes and identifying evidence that will be accepted as a means of determining that the objective has been achieved. Sometimes it is necessary to go into some detail by describing how well the students must perform or to what degree evidence must exist for you to know that the performance intent was fulfilled. Be sure to write as many descriptive statements as are needed to specify the intended outcome.

MANAGERIAL PERFORMANCE CONTRACTS

Some school systems have adopted a more simplified approach to performance accountability by writing objectives in performance contract form. The West Hartford, Connecticut, and Madison, Wisconsin, school systems use this simplified but successful approach.

The middle manager (usually the school principal) signs a performance commitment to accomplish certain objectives within a specified time frame. This approach does not involve the detailed steps described in this book. The contract is between the middle manager and his immediate superior.

The objectives are stated in measurable terms. A specified time of accomplishment is stated.

Through courtesy of Superintendent Charles O. Richter of the West Hartford Public Schools, a sample managerial performance objective will be found on page 180.

THE NEED FOR CLEARLY
UNDERSTOOD OUTCOMES

The author recently participated in a discussion with three professors from the same college department who taught a course that was required of all students seeking to graduate from that department. In the discussion it was agreed that this one course focused upon one of the two or three most essential performance outcomes of the entire department. It was agreed that the very reason for the existence of the department rested largely upon the results anticipated from the instruction in this critical and fundamental course. As the discussion led to the objectives of this course and as the author attempted to tie down the specific performance outcomes it became evident to all four of us that the three professors had somewhat divergent interpretations concerning the performance intent. The professors agreed that students should be able to enroll in the course under any instructor and receive, by and large, quite similar instruction that would result in some very definite performance skills. It was agreed that if these skills were missing students would have considerable difficulty throughout the remainder of the course work to be taken in this department. If these three professors were to sit down to write a performance objective there would be widely divergent differences in the statements.

A further discussion of this interesting situation in this particular college department revealed that a syllabus had been written to guide the course of instruction and to make sure that there would be reasonably identical student performance outcomes. An examination of the syllabus, however, soon identified the problem. Loaded and ambiguous words were used. The existence of quantifiable language in the syllabus was almost nil. Highly specialized individuals holding doctorates in this discipline interpreted key descriptive phrases differently. The situation was almost tantamount to a number of construction workers building the same house while reading different blueprints.

Management owes students and teachers in education better explanations and descriptions of performance expectations than those demonstrated in the above example. This situation, however, is quite typical of many problems in education today. We need to do a better job of describing where we are going and of making sure that numerous persons are reading the same road maps and traveling in the same direction.

Following are two examples of written objectives intended to improve handwriting in two different elementary schools. These are contrasting examples of objectives written for the same academic year but with obvious differences in meeting the criteria discussed in this chapter for concise and quantifiable language:

Example Number One:

All faculty members in grades four through six will concentrate on handwriting improvement. Students will be encouraged to take more interest and have more pride in the legibility of their handwriting. Handwriting will be emphasized in all subjects in the school curriculum.

Example Number Two:

By April 30, 1974, at least 85% of the students enrolled in this school will be able to write legibly according to the Handwriting Scale established by Nobel and Nobel (1960).

While neither of these objectives is an ideal example, the first example is a statement that the school is going to try to improve handwriting. The statement aspires to encourage more interest and more pride in handwriting. But it does not specify when this will be accomplished or what criterion measures will be used.

In example two, this objective is much more precise. A time certain is specified for all staff members to understand. A well-known handwriting scale is specified as the criterion against which accomplishment will be measured. Faculty and students committed to the attainment of this objective can get the handwriting scale and use it as a standard of excellence in measuring performance accomplishment.

Most written objectives used in an MBO system specify a time certain when outcomes will be attained. It is as important to say *when* as it is to say *what*. While most objectives are adopted for an academic year it does help to specify when what is to be accomplished.

Some objectives are simple and can be stated very concisely with a few descriptive sentences. The objective on handwriting given above will not require complex elaboration as a guide for performance accountability. However, some major problems in education are very complex and are extremely difficult to solve without a network of sub-objectives requiring the performance attention of various units in the system. In such circumstances the major objective is stated with further elaboration given in a series of sub-objectives. Some sub-objectives are contingent upon the accomplishment of other specified outcomes. Some aspects of work to be accomplished cannot be begun until other sub-objectives have been attained. This gets into more sophisticated planning and performance accountability practices. Such things are beyond the scope of this book, but the need for sub-objectives on a much simpler scale can be met by beginners involved in first experiences with MBO.

PROBLEM DESCRIPTIONS

Drawing from the facts gained from the needs assessment program and utilizing the performance priority statements issued by the chief executive officer of the institution, problem descriptions are usually written as a prelude to the statement of a major objective. The problem description identifies the need. It usually provides some interesting data that describe the gap between what is and what should be in the performance of the school or department.

The problem description that introduces a statement of a major objective should not be long and elaborate. Usually a descriptive statement of three or four paragraphs accompanied by substantiating data will suffice in describing the problem and the background purposes for the major objective.

The following is an example of a problem description developed in the Bureau of Higher Education of the U. S. Office of Education in justification of implementing a major objective related to the education of economically disadvantaged students:

The Problem

The relationships of family income and educational attainment are apparent in that: students coming from families earning $7,500 or less constitute 43% of the elementary school enrollment but only 28.8% of the college enrollment; 15% of the students whose family income was below $3,000 failed to graduate from high school while for those whose family income was $15,000 or higher only 5.3% failed to graduate; and 46% of the low income children are likely to attend educational institutions having per-student expenditures below the national average while only 10% attend schools where expenditures are above the national average. Assuming instructional expenditures per child are indicative of educational quality, low income students are then most likely to receive an education of inferior quality.

Inequalities in educational experience and attainment have consequences for future earning. Data indicates that men who completed less than eight years of school had a mean income of $4,100; men who completed high school $8,400; and men who completed four years of college $12,200.

Approximately 18 million adults in the U. S. are unable to read and write well enough to fill out business forms needed by banks, the Social Security Administration, and the Internal Revenue Service. In addition, one percent of the high school leavers are at or below literacy levels. Grade level attainment is a poor predictor of literacy as shown by a special sample that read at the fourth grade level but had an eleventh grade education. Officially, the literacy rate is 99% but functionally literacy may be as low as 82 to 85%.

The above problem description was followed by an objective written by this bureau in the U. S. Office of Education. Since the objective specifies certain performance intent that will be accomplished within the time frames of a fiscal year, it is important for the problem description to make the objective more meaningful and help all members of the team understand the urgency for striving to accomplish the objective.

Some problem descriptions can be very brief and still state the reason for the objective that is adopted as part of the management system for the coming year. An example of this is the following description written by the faculty of the East Mill Creek School in the Granite School District of Salt Lake City:

Problem Description

Legibility in handwriting in both formal training and application has been a major concern to the faculty of this school during the past year. We have found that more than 25% of our children have deficiencies that are below the minimum acceptable standards. This weakness naturally handicaps the students in recording their ideas with fluency. It also limits communication effectiveness.

In the above problem description the need for the objective in handwriting improvement is quantified. The statement calling attention to the need should help all members of the faculty to realize that there is some urgency in correcting the situation.

In many instances, the problem description that precedes the statement of the major objective summarizes information attained from the needs assessment project. It reflects the concern of the local institution or department and identifies the extent to which a certain institution-wide deficiency identified in the performance priority descriptions exists on this level of operation.

ADOPTION PROCEDURE

If a major objective is to receive the total attention and support of all members of the faculty it must be recognized as a matter of urgent concern and high priority. This consensus in accepting an objective should not be difficult to achieve if the faculty members were meaningfully involved in the needs assessment program. Further consensus should also have been attained when the preliminary performance priorities were issued by the chief executive officer as outlined in Chapter 3 of this book. In both instances the faculty should have been extensively involved in lively discussion and debate centered around the endeavors of the institution. This discussion should focus on what efforts will be of the most worth and what problems are in greatest need of solution.

The procedure for adopting objectives also must involve the participation of the staff. If they come to this point having had a voice in needs assessment and in refining the institution wide performance priorities there should be high interest and considerable readiness for the task of adopting objectives.

Administrators must avoid having the operational objectives identified as theirs. The objectives to which the school or department will be focusing financial and personnel resources must be those that have wide acceptance and general consensus as high priority concerns worthy of the attention of the total staff.

FINAL REVIEW AND APPROVAL

Once the objectives have been agreed upon and after they have been written, revised as an outgrowth of extensive feedback and discussion, and rewritten in final form they are ready to be submitted to the central office of the institution or school system. In the central office the objectives should be reviewed to see that they are responsive to the performance priorities.

They should be studied to determine if they can be realistically attained within the limits of the resources of the institution and the resources of the school or department from whence they came. Need for coordination over department lines and for elimination of overlap and duplication should be noted in the central office processing of the written objectives from the various units that comprise the total institution or school system. The scope and depth of some objectives may need to be reduced because of other priority demands. The central office must have a voice in matters such as these since it is from this vantage point that the total needs and the total resources can be taken into account in the appraisal and determination of practicality.

Once this processing in the central office has been accomplished the units are given the green light to proceed with operation plans and time-phased action steps to attain the performance outcomes. Approval of the objectives from the central office constitutes a performance commitment. The actual blueprint from results-oriented management is beginning to take shape. In the central office will be kept the total objectives of all the units in the system or institution and identification of how the objectives will relate to the performance priorities previously adopted by the chief executive officer. The quantified and time-phased statements will make it possible to measure progress in terms of concrete results.

LIMITING THE NUMBER OF MAJOR OBJECTIVES

Most MBO systems encourage limitation of the number of major objectives during an operational planning period to from six to twelve major performance outcomes. These objectives are special priorities. The units in the organization must not only carry the burden of meeting these performance measures, but must also accomplish the ordinary and usual ongoing workload. Experience has shown that when a unit exceeds a load of twelve major objectives the system begins to break down because of the weight of the commitment and the pressure of the demands for extra effort. As a school system or university is learning to manage by objectives the number should be limited to possibly three to five major performance commitments. After the learning experience the number of objectives may be increased to as many as twelve.

From the central management viewpoint a large and complex school system or university will have a large number of objectives to monitor when the outside limit is set at twelve. Going much beyond this could create a burden of complexity and volume that cannot be handled. The follow-through and execution techniques described in subsequent chapters of this book will, the author believes, convince the reader of the wisdom of limiting the number of major performance objectives to a few in each unit. Limiting performance objectives is often found to be difficult in large organizations. Each segment of the educational bureaucracy has its own pet projects and priorities. Each professor or teacher understandably has a special interest in an area of individual concern. Usually there is intense competition to have a particular special interest identified as a sufficiently high priority to merit the special management consideration that comes with MBO. This means that some very worthy outcomes will have to be delayed in deference to some that are identified as more worthwhile. This calls for a certain amount of give and take inside the units of the organization. School principals and department heads in colleges are often hard pressed to cope with the intense competition that emerges once the various factions and special interests realize that MBO gets results. There is keen competition and a certain amount of politicking that goes on inside an organization after the results-oriented potential of MBO gains full recognition by all the staff.

This rivalry or competition to have objectives adopted can be very wholesome and beneficial to the institution if it is utilized properly. It certainly eliminates pet projects that cannot stand the total scrutiny of the entire staff. Lame excuses and ill-founded priorities are smoked out and put in their proper place. All of this leads to improved morale as decisions are based upon the facts. Management inefficiency and administrative cowardice are often identified in the objective-adopting procedure of an educational institution that has committed itself to an MBO style of operation.

The written objectives set forth in the concise style and format advocated in this chapter place the total educational institution on a performance accountability footing where results take precedence over rhetoric and where performance gets some long overdue consideration ahead of personality and institutional politics.

SUMMARY

In this chapter we have discussed performance objectives as a means of making specific commitments to attain certain quantifiable results. We have emphasized the importance of communicating performance intent in the writing of objectives. We have also stressed the need for the objectives to be stated in quantifiable terms. The objective must be measurable if we are to successfully manage in a way that will result in its accomplishment. We have described the procedure for central office adoption of objectives and have strongly advocated broad staff involvement so that consensus and commitment will be attained.

In the next chapter we will discuss the formulation of time-phased action steps and how to execute the detail of operational planning as a prelude to actual implementation of operational management by objectives.

5

Time-Phased Action Steps: The Products of Operational Planning

This chapter deals with the implementation of the objectives described in Chapter 4. At this phase in establishing a school management by objectives program, planning for the actual implementation of work to accomplish the objectives adopted by each unit of the educational institution will be described. The setting up of time-phased milestones and action steps and the scheduling of such resources as staff time and money will be treated in some detail. This chapter will be devoted to the operational planning phase of the program and will describe how action steps are established and assigned to key members of the staff.

TIME-PHASED ACTION STEPS

In its broadest sense operational planning includes all of the planning that goes into management by objectives. Technically, therefore, operational planning includes the steps described in the preceding chapters. Many managers have come to accept the idea that commitments to specific action steps are necessary to accomplish a particular objective. In planning for management of the day-by-day efforts that in sum total will cause a major objective to be accomplished it is necessary to describe in some detail what is to be done and who is to do it. Therefore, operational planning as the term is used in this book will refer to the establishment in writing of certain specific action steps that must be accomplished by a time certain on the program calendar if an essential aspect of an objective is to be accomplished.

The purpose of operational planning is to take a major objective, analyze the important details of the work to be done, estimate the time and resources required to do it, and assign specific staff members unambiguous responsibilities in seeing that essential action steps are accomplished within the time available. Operational planning fixes performance responsibility within a unit of a large educational institution. It states very simply *who is to do what by when.*

Another important function of operational planning is to permit the staff to think through the steps that must be taken and to anticipate those action steps that have to be accomplished before other phases of the total work can be begun. This facilitates staff coordination and staff awareness of the necessity for teamwork. It allows sub-units of the college department or school unit in a school system to synchronize their efforts to the mutual advantage of all units in the organization.

It must be kept in mind that operational planning will not represent all or possibly even a major portion of the total activities of the staff. Rather, operational planning will set forth the *special* tasks to which the staff has committed itself in order to accomplish the high priority objective that the unit of the educational institution has promised to accomplish as part of the total institutional team effort. The action steps in the operational plan represent results that staff members have committed themselves to attain within a specified time frame regardless of the other demands upon their time and their resources.

Operational planning does not concern itself with things that will happen automatically without special management attention. The operational planning process confines itself to those activities where a specific amount of management attention will be required to make the difference in accomplishment that will be essential to reach a certain milestone event of attainment by a specified and necessary time.

Operational planning must address itself to questions of feasibility and reasonableness. There should be reasonable assurance that with hard work a specific outcome essential to the attainment of the major objective can actually be achieved within the amount of time and the confines of the resources available. Likewise, operational planning should concern itself with making sure that there is sufficient challenge in the work accomplishment commitments that are set forth in the operational planning process. If the task is too simplistic and easy it will not be worthwhile. The entire purpose of school management by objectives is to set forth a special commitment of effort to attain a highly desirable and very important outcome. Therefore, the details of the work plan must be challenging to the staff and still be within the realm of feasibility of accomplishment.

TIME-PHASED MILESTONES

The total staff of the school or college department should sit down together and discuss strategy for implementing work action to accomplish a major objective to which the unit has made commitment for a special effort of accomplishment during the academic year. Since the staff was involved in needs assessment, reaction, criticism, and revision of the chief executive officer's performance priorities, and since the staff assisted in the actual adoption of a list of major operational objectives for the school or department, there should be no time spent at this phase of the program in discussing major commitments. These have already been made and have been submitted to the chief executive officer and his staff for review and approval. Therefore, the staff should be discussing the *how*, the *who*, and the *when* of implementation. *Since the commitment has been made at this point the discussion centers on how to get it done and not on whether it is worthwhile doing.*

As the staff meets together in brainstorming sessions a broad array of alternative strategies for solving a major problem should be set down for critical examination. New, creative, and sometimes unorthodox approaches should be brought out. Past experience should be applied in trying to project what the ultimate consequences might be from following different avenues in attacking problems. The question asked numerous times should be whether there are other possibilities or alternative approaches or entirely new directions that should be examined before launching forth into the day-to-day activity of getting the problem solved and the major objective accomplished. *The staff should not be satisfied with a one-solution approach but should examine thoroughly and challenge vigorously all of the assumptions until there is satisfaction and general consensus that the best possible strategy has been identified.*

After the staff has had adequate time to thoroughly analyze alternative approaches to solving the problem represented by the major objective, some milestone events of accomplishment should be projected throughout the course of the academic year. These milestone events should be stated in time phase so that the entire staff will be aware of the fact that deadlines are approaching and certain things have to be done by certain times in the year. Other action steps in the work should be planned as a means of reaching additional major milestones that constitute the roadmap of accomplishment to get to the end result specified in the objective. These time-phased milestone events of accomplishment and the action steps that lead up to each of them comprise the basic framework for the total operational planning system. Most MBO systems attempt to show in chart form the action steps and the time requirements to attain certain milestones of accomplishment. These charts are useful in monitoring progress as described in Chapter 4. The chart forms and accompanying information used in the Granite School System MBO program are presented in Appendix D of this book.

Inexperienced staff members will have considerable difficulty with the development of the operational plans that set forth the necessary milestone events of accomplishment and the action steps leading to them. It is a difficult job to imaginatively project through a total year of work to reach a major objective. Adjustments in certain time-phased commitments are inevitable, and much frustration can be avoided if it is made clear to the staff that not all action steps require precise estimates of the time of accomplishments. It is also important to make clear that many time projections for beginners must be best guesses until experience can be applied.

The author noticed a high degree of over-aspiration in the first year that the staff of a large school district attempted to implement the details of operational planning as a guide to work accomplishments. It was interesting to note that in the subsequent year most of the time-phased estimates were very close to reality. Staff planners gave adequate time for accomplishment of the action steps without under-committing and underestimating. Contrary to common belief, most staff members do not deliberately underestimate and under-aspire when a management by objectives system places time-phased operational planning programs before them. The inclination is, according to the author's experience, more toward over-aspiration than to under-aspiration.

While sophisticated systems planners utilize PERT or other network planning and projection systems, the beginner in MBO should utilize a simple time-phased chart (such as the one found in Appendix D) with a few easily understood symbols to show major milestone events of accomplishment and action steps.

SCHEDULING COMMITMENTS OF STAFF, PHYSICAL FACILITIES, AND MONEY

The entire purpose of management by objectives is to attain performance accountability, to set priorities and marshal resources on a rational, priority basis, and to solve major problems of great significance to the educational institution. This cannot be done without establishing the conditions necessary to accomplishment of the worthy purposes represented in the major objectives. This means that the front office must allocate staff, physical facilities, and dollars to support the unit committed to high priority work. This allocation often means painful reallocation of staff, physical facilities, and money. But this reallocation usually brings about a higher order of thinking, planning, and executing. The institution becomes performance conscious. This begets awareness of waste of both time and money. Some bad situations that have been tolerated for a long time become intolerable when all of the staff become involved in thinking, planning, and priority setting.

Attendant to the action steps and the accomplishment of the major milestone events must be the commitments when the "who does what" question is answered. Most of the action-step charts in the operational planning system list a key staff person by name on the chart where an action step is presented. In situations where materials, equipment, and special items must be purchased a dollar amount is also placed on the chart so that the staff member committed to the action step has assurance that he has the means of getting the work done. This is where administrative accountability comes into the picture.

Many action steps in the operational planning process require no additional dollars but merely time commitment. In fact, some operational planning systems yield added dollars that are made available for some other high priority purpose. The emphasis upon output and the results-oriented aspect of this type of management results in savings as well as expenditures.

The wise administrator utilizes the democratic process of participation and sharing as dollar and staff time commitments are made. The result is actually beneficial to the executive because staff members tend to discipline each other. False and erroneous assumptions are smoked out and identified for what they are. Where difficult and unpopular staff assignments have to be made there is better understanding and higher morale if extensive involvement has prevailed throughout the entire process. More understanding and sympathy for the task that a principal or department head has to face will be apparent when these tough decisions are made openly before the entire group. Another important byproduct of staff involvement in scheduling commitments of staff time and money is the fact that all staff members have an opportunity to think about and analyze cost and effectiveness. Some outcomes may be attained on schedule and executed with great precision. Some others will obviously not be worth the time and money spent on them. When such facts are weighed under the light of total staff scrutiny, performance accountability comes into its own. Obvious high cost and low benefit projects often meet an early but timely death when brought out into the total view of the entire staff of a school or college department. This causes management to be accountable to the staff as well as the staff to management.

Inequities in regular work loads are examined when the total staff participates in the special time commitments that are demanded by the action steps contained in the operational plans of an MBO system. Since the accomplishment of most objectives will require special effort and since the ongoing activity must not be abandoned, staff time priority considerations are weighed carefully. A healthy dialogue comes from open examination by the staff of questions concerning who should be assigned to make sure that a specific action step is accomplished. Some staff members' so-called easy jobs do not turn out to be so easy and, contrary-wise, some staff members' reputed-to-be difficult jobs turn out to be less difficult as a result of the process of participatory decision making of staff time commitment to action steps in the MBO system.

6

Operational Management and Execution of Action Step Plans

In this chapter operational management of the time-phased action steps will be discussed. The reader will be taken through the management review conference process. We will discuss how performance failure is diagnosed. We will describe what steps should be taken under MBO to get the operational plan on the track so that the major objectives can be reached. The process of keeping a continuous management dialogue and of reporting progress will be discussed in some detail. This chapter treats the topic of performance accountability through coordination and constant leadership that will gain teamwork and keep the momentum of the organization moving down the road toward full realization of the objectives that have been adopted.

REPORTING PROGRESS

The large and complex educational organization must avoid over-complicating and over-sophisticating the function of managers. Management by objectives simplifies by identifying in the detail described in Chapters 4 and 5 of this book the most important problems to be solved during an academic year. It calls attention to work priorities.

If properly executed, the institution will have arrived at this point with a broad consensus and a universal commitment to reach certain very important performance outcomes before the academic year expires. At this point in the MBO cycle the school system or university has identified its most pressing problems, has written in measurable terms the objectives and performance outcomes to be attained in solving these problems, and has completed some very crucial operational planning work that has resulted in some time-phased action steps that will tell the key persons in the organization specifically what is to be accomplished, how it is to be done and when it is to be completed. We are ready for the execution of the details from operational planning.

Most MBO systems break down at this juncture in the program of attaining performance accountability. Communication beyond this point seems to fade away if continuous attention is not drawn to the performance commitments that were made. Part of this difficulty stems from the fact that the regular operational program has to be executed in addition to the accomplishment of the major objectives identified as those problems for which special effort will be made. The total student body is on board and the usual teaching and learning activity must be accomplished. The key managers get bogged down in the routine of seeing the system get itself through the academic year. While MBO should not cause the educational system to be dominated by its own mechanics or to follow recipes of performance so slavishly as to obstruct and overregulate, there must be some agreed-upon checkpoints at which time the key managers and the persons assigned to vital roles in accomplishing the time-phased action steps get together to talk about problems and progress.

The reporting of progress and accomplishing the action steps developed in the MBO system can usually be accomplished without a heavy paperwork burden. As certain milestone events are reached the key administrators should provide the quantitative and qualitative information that will describe the progress to that point. This should be committed to writing, but the report should be simple, terse, and factual. The reporting language should reflect the quantifiable terms that were described in Chapter 4 of this book. The persons to whom responsibilities were distributed as described in Chapter 5 will be the persons making simple reports to the managers with whom they have made the performance commitments. These reports will express themselves in terms of results measured against the established objectives. If the objectives were simple, quantifiable, and stated in common language the reports can be brief, factual, and free from wordy rhetoric.

MANAGEMENT REVIEW CONFERENCES

The literature on management by objectives as applied to industry strongly suggests that the chief executive officer sit down at least once every month with each of the key managers of major sub-units in his organization to receive an oral report and to participate in a lively dialogue on the progress of the organization. The author has found this practice to be especially valuable in a large school system. After MBO has been well established in a large institution it should be reasonably self-regulating and self-operating so that only exceptional problems and unusual situations need to be treated in management review conferences.

As they meet in the management review conference, the chief executive officer should make sure that a non-threatening posture is assumed. He must be ready to praise and recognize accomplishment at the same time that he expresses concern that certain time-phased action steps have not been met. In discussing the latter, he must assume some responsibility for failure to reach certain milestones of accomplishment since conditions are usually far from optimum and ideal because of limited resources and other problems beyond the control of the unit head. So, as the chief executive and the head of a major unit sit down together to review the performance stewardship, the conference table should be surrounded with an atmosphere of mutual trust and concern and a feeling of openness and non-defensiveness on the part of the unit head. If this atmosphere prevails it will be largely a product of the administrative behavior of the chief executive officer. More will be said about this in subsequent chapters.

As the chief executive officer holds his monthly management review conference his staff should place before him the problem descriptions, the major operational objectives, the products of the operational planning effort of the unit he is reviewing, and a chart containing the time-phased action steps to which the unit has committed itself. It will then be a simple matter for the chief executive and his unit head to go over the performance commitments, review the major milestone events and check the time-phased action steps. By moving briefly through the list of events that should have been reached, a quick inventory of accomplishment can be taken. Typically, a number of action steps will have been completed ahead of schedule and some will be lagging behind the time commitments that were made.

In the Granite School System the form shown in Figure 1 is used to record the most important action steps and milestones of accomplishment. An examination of this form will reveal its value as a ready reference for the use of the chief executive in the management review conference. He can tell at a glance what work was scheduled to be initiated, in progress, and completed according to the unit's operational plan. This form provides the basis for management dialogue.

Except in unusual circumstances it has been generally found to be a very productive and rewarding practice to have a few key staff members sitting in at the management review conference. Usually the unit head will not have all the details and will not have available in his own mind sufficient background to answer all the questions that the chief executive officer may want to ask. Therefore, persons key to the performance outcomes that will be reviewed should be available to describe the program and identify the problems that are being confronted. This involvement of a number of key persons is beneficial from both directions. The chief executive officer has an opportunity to get acquainted

GRANITE SCHOOL DISTRICT
340 EAST 3545 SOUTH • SALT LAKE CITY, UTAH 84115
Telephone 801

Name of School_____

Administrative Complex_____

Principal_____

MBO Form B--Time Phased Action Steps to Attain Major Objectives or
                Significant Sub-Objectives
                (To be used to monitor progress in MBO)

In the form below list the detailed action steps to be executed in accomplishing the objective or sub-objective. The following symbols will denote beginning dates and completion dates for each action step:

     ④————————————————/13\

   ○   = month and day action step is initiated.

   △   = month and day action step is completed.

————— = the line shows the duration of activity from initiation to completion.

Action Steps	Staff Member Responsible	M O N T H S												Explanation and more detail on page # attached
		J	A	S	O	N	D	J	F	M	A	M	J	

                                                   Page #_____

FIGURE 1

with and listen to reports from individuals with whom he would not normally have contact. The staff members working with the unit head have an opportunity to gain an institution-wide perspective from the chief executive officer. Many misunderstandings are avoided and great gaps in management communication are closed at these management review conferences. The greater the involvement the more effective will be the communication.

It is very important that monthly management review conferences be held when scheduled. They should be brief, succinct, factual, and carried out in an atmosphere of total candor. The chief executive can set the tone by moving through the management review agenda very quickly with the conversation focusing on the critical points that need attention. If the conferences are to be held regularly and without undue burden upon busy staff members and administrators they must be brief, businesslike, and free from redundant conversation. Management review conferences that drag on over long periods of time lead to skips and postponements in subsequent months and the whole MBO process will start to break down. This continuous dialogue is vital to an organization that is dynamically committed to institutional renewal and progress. Brevity and businesslike following of the management review agenda will accomplish the major purpose of the conferences without placing a heavy time burden upon anyone.

At the conclusion of the management review conference the chief executive officer should be quite familiar with the operational problems and progress of the unit that he is reviewing. His staff and key staff members from the unit head should have a good understanding about the steps to be taken in executing activities that will continue to advance the unit to the ultimate realization of its major objectives for the academic year.

Some plans may have to be put in motion to recover lost time. Some details of executing operational programs to accomplish certain objectives may have to be modified in the middle of the academic year. Some resources may have to be deployed or some specific aspects of certain objectives may have to be modified so that the staff members will have a reasonable chance to reach their objectives. Above all, the chief executive officer should not try to force a unit to unreasonable effort just because the staff may have over-aspired or underestimated accomplishment capacities. The conference should end with a good understanding of what is to be accomplished during the next month prior to the next conference. With some emphasis upon encouragement and recognition for work well done, the management review conference should end with all concerned having a can-do attitude and an optimistic outlook. This is particularly important during the first year of experience in MBO.

MANAGEMENT BY EXCEPTION

As is well known by experienced administrators the best laid plans can often go awry because of circumstances beyond the control of management. Staff resignations, unanticipated enrollment increases or decreases, passage of new laws or court interpretations of old laws may all affect the accomplishment of a major objective during an academic year. Long established rules of procedure may suddenly be found unworkable because of one or more of the above-mentioned unanticipated developments. All of this emphasizes the fact that exceptions must be made in recognition of unusual events that may happen. A rule or long established operation practice may be generally applicable to most units and individuals in the organization while being obviously unfair or ill advised for others. Without being too capricious or arbitrary, key managers must administer MBO programs with sufficient wisdom to recognize that exceptions must be made. This applies to students, individual staff members, or units in the total educational institution. If contingencies are anticipated as much as possible during the planning process, the management-by-exception action will be well accepted by all concerned because of the obvious fairness and reasonableness of granting exceptions.

The use of a management system should not excuse rigidity on the part of managers. Indeed, a good management system will facilitate rather than obstruct adaptability to unusual and unforeseen circumstances. MBO need not be rigid and inflexible. In fact, the wide involvement advocated in this book of all staff members will tend to combat rigidity and oppressiveness in management. No place will this be more evident than in the operational management and execution of action steps.

MONITORING AND DIAGNOSING PERFORMANCE FAILURE

By clearly identifying who does what, performance responsibilities are fixed and failure to perform according to specifications can be more easily diagnosed. Major milestone events of accomplishment are indicated in the documents prepared during the operational planning steps described in Chapter 5.

In the actual execution of the action steps of MBO, managers will be anticipating these milestone events, will know that the same will be discussed in monthly management review conferences. They will be lending encouragement and placing support behind staff members in a way that enhances the probability of success. In this sense, performance failure is often failure of the staff team, including the key managers.

THE GRAPEVINE MONITORING SYSTEM

The scheduling of these major milestone events of accomplishment leads to anticipation of certain specified results by a deadline date. With all eyes on these deadlines, performance failure can often be foreseen and averted. When performance outcomes are specified and performance accountability is fixed upon certain individuals to attain certain ends by a completion deadline, the conversation of staff members at coffee breaks, in the lunch room, and in other places around the campus centers upon these anticipated accomplishments. Out of this lively dialogue related to objectives that were adopted through involvement of the total staff comes an informal but effective monitoring system. A staff member upon whose shoulders rests a heavy responsibility is often asked how he is doing or what the chances are that he will not make his deadline. This grapevine monitoring system often diagnoses performance difficulties far enough in advance to make it possible to change the game plan and execute some recovery steps. The informal, grapevine type of monitoring system is only effective if the MBO system is accepted by the total staff as their program and their commitment. Therefore, the more genius used by management in getting staff involvement and commitment during the planning process the more effective will be the informal and unofficial monitoring system.

During staff meeting and in the process of other ongoing operational contacts the school principal or college department head will have numerous opportunities to check on progress in executing plans in the MBO system. The administrator can casually refer to some concerns that he may have or make inquiry as to how things are going. Additionally, individuals or groups making up a particular staff team should be contacted regularly to receive encouragement and to give progress reports that will prognosticate accomplishment probabilities. If the leadership behavior is positive and non-threatening the entire process of diagnosing performance failure and monitoring accomplishment will be executed in an atmosphere of helpfulness and supportiveness. In this regard, wise leaders learn the difference between pressure and creative tension in an organization. The requisite conditions for success must be created by the administrators. *Encouragement and positive reinforcement should then lead the staff to do its best in an organization that is long on encouragement and short on blame fixing and recrimination.*

CONTINUOUS MANAGEMENT DIALOGUE AND COMMUNICATION

Effective and continuous communication is one of the biggest problems in large educational organizations such as big city school systems and large universities. MBO, if properly executed, should facilitate communication by forcing a constant dialogue on various levels and between numerous departments in the educational institution. This communication should be relevant and sincerely centered upon performance problems and performance outcomes. Both the formal and informal as well as the official and unofficial communication systems should be engaged in the process of executing the action steps in operationally managing certain objectives during the academic year.

Poor communication begets low morale, confusion, and strife. Effective communication will actually happen only if the administrators openly and candidly address themselves to the relevant problems.

Administrative failure must be forthrightly admitted. If an action step is fumbled because management failed to meet certain commitments and to create conditions essential to success, the first step in getting things back on the track is for the administration to concede openly that they fumbled the ball and to then take necessary action to recover. This approach is vital to good communication. Administrative failure is often well known to the entire staff and the atmosphere can be cleared quickly if management will be the first to bring the matter up, accept the justifiable criticism, and then turn to the future.

Unwholesome and counter-productive rivalries between individuals and among various factions on school and college campuses often obstruct progress and damage learning opportunities for students. Continuous management dialogue and communication will tend to decrease these abrasive circumstances. Administrators should look for opportunities to casually raise issues that exist between individuals and bring about wholesome communication in openness and candor so that gaps of misunderstanding can be bridged, and apologies and explanations for certain behavior offered. Particularly in education is this interpersonal climate among staff members important. The openness of MBO and the need to continuously share problems, concede mistakes, and seek help from each other will tend to create this desirable wholesomeness of interpersonal relationship. Many rivalries and conflicts linger on for long periods of time when simple communication could heal hurt feelings and correct misapprehensions and misplaced motives. During the operational management phase of executing the MBO program, wise administrators will utilize opportunities to mend the climate of relationships.

Communication among units such as individual schools in a school system or separate departments on a university campus can also be facilitated out of the management dialogue that must take place in MBO. Institutional rivalry and misunderstanding are also problems with which top level administrators must cope. MBO provides opportunities for units in an educational institution to reach out to each other with assistance and mutually advantageous cooperation. The chief executive officer will find growing out of his management review conferences many opportunities to build sound inter-unit relationships that will result in overall efficiency of the total organization.

During the academic year, as the staff members of the various units of the institution are executing the action steps, particular attention should be called to highlights in the progress being attained to reach the objectives adopted. This will generate consciousness of MBO and awareness that all the members of the staff have made commitments to attain some very large and significant performance outcomes during the academic year.

If little attention is called through the normal communications channels, the MBO effort will not be considered important in the minds of the staff. Through a continuous management dialogue and through emphasizing the fact that special projects are underway to meet some of the most critical needs, the total MBO program will begin to permeate the thinking of those individuals who make a difference in helping the institution renew itself and grow to newer heights of performance accomplishment.

SUMMARY

In this chapter the significance of reporting and monitoring progress in executing the time-phased action steps of MBO has been discussed. The value of management review conferences and the necessity of holding them regularly were stressed. The need to involve staff members in management review conferences along with unit heads and the benefit to be derived in meeting regularly with the chief executive officer and his staff to report on progress and problems were described. The role of effective communications in executing MBO action steps and the particular value of the grapevine type of communications network were pointed out. The need to manage by exception and to make adaptations to plans and time schedules was emphasized in connection with the well-known fact that unanticipated changes require a certain amount of flexibility and adaptability to new circumstances.

The author found the management review conferences to be sources of information for improving his own effectiveness as a superintendent of schools. Principals are able to report problems and identify areas where central office staff members are failing to provide the necessary support. The conferences are useful to the unit heads. They, too, can identify performance failure. They have a forum in which to air concerns and grievances.

The management review conference must be conducted in a manner that will encourage and permit criticism to flow from the bottom up as well as from the top down. If this actually happens it will result from the approach of non-threatening openness on the part of the chief executive officer. All participants must attack the problems and not each other. If the executive in charge insists on it, the staff members from the unit being reviewed will leave the conference feeling that they had full opportunity to explain and to offer suggestions as to how others might help them to succeed.

Particularly important in this chapter has been the emphasis given to the actual execution of the MBO effort in a climate that is as non-threatening as possible. In this phase of the MBO cycle will exist ample opportunity for the application of authoritarian and negative pressures. For this reason the opposite potential of building a truly democratic system that will enhance morale and create a genuine attitude of commitment received more than the usual amount of attention. More on building morale through MBO and on gaining staff involvement and participative management will be covered in Chapter 7.

7

Staff Involvement and Participative Management: Keys to High Morale and Commitment

This chapter will discuss the principles and techniques for gaining staff involvement and commitment to MBO. The author has experienced a somewhat negative response from professional colleagues to the practices, described in the previous chapters, wherein objectives are identified and performance commitments are made to fix specific responsibility upon individuals to attain certain outcomes by specified deadlines. This system can become a tool for pressure and highhanded management on the part of administrators. But it actually has more potential for giving all staff members an opportunity to have a voice in managing the school system or university. These possibilities and suggestions as to how they may be realized will be covered here.

MBO IS NOT A "BIG BROTHER IS WATCHING" SYSTEM

Dr. H. Merrell Arnold, assistant professor of management at the University of Wisconsin, recently defined management by objectives as follows:

Simply stated, management by objectives is a pattern of supervision by which the areas of responsibility for an individual are
reviewed and the results to be achieved are pre-determined as
accurately as possible. Normally these objectives are stated by
the subordinate, but they are not authentic until approved by
the supervisor. In all cases they are written so there will be no
question as to what the individual's goals were at the time of
the performance appraisal.*

Dr. Arnold goes on to discuss his definition of management
by objectives with the following:

There are three questions that must be capable of appropriate
answers by the majority of members if any organization is to
be effective:

(1) What results are expected of me?
(2) What level of performance is considered successful?
(3) How am I doing in relation to those standards of
performance?

A potent MBO program will make any school manager capable
of dealing with all three of these questions.

When professional educators read definitions and explanations such as the one quoted above from Dr. Arnold, apprehensions begin to rise and questions concerning whether MBO might
be offensive to professionals come up. It should be stated unequivocally that MBO is not a scheme to develop a "Big Brother
Is Watching" system with shades of Orwell's *1984.* Indeed, MBO
should lead to the opposite direction. Based upon his own experience, the author believes that MBO puts more pressure on
administrators to attain performance accountability than it does
upon the teaching staff. The performance commitments of MBO
require a higher order of administrative skill. Leadership failure
stands out under an MBO system where responsibility is fixed and
performance commitments are made before operations begin.

ACCOUNTABILITY BEGINS AT THE TOP

Contrary to common belief performance accountability begins at the top. The administrator must be the facilitator and

*Arnold, H. Merrill, "Management by Objectives and the School System," *The School
Administrator,* American Association of School Administrators, pp. 15-16, February, 1972.

expeditor of action steps. Most of his time will be spent in attaining coordination and facilitating understanding and free-flowing communication. He will have less time to perform the "Big Brother" role than was available under the traditional system. Additionally, the administrator who is inclined to abuse his authority will find this behavior more unacceptable and more subject to staff criticism under MBO than ordinarily is the case. He cannot operate with a hidden agenda and the technique of playing various factions against each other (so well known as the trademark of weak administrative leadership) will stand out for immediate attack under MBO.

The management system advocated in this book is not, however, a panacea for the ailments of weak and petty administrative practice. MBO will make good administrators stronger and it will most definitely identify the causes and root sources of administrative malfunction. The faculty that has no alternative but to endure in silence the vicissitudes of weak and petty leadership can easily put together a bill of particulars to place before principal, dean, or college department head after MBO has been in operation for a year. The documentation of performance expectations as advocated in MBO will, the author believes, tend to eliminate both the authoritarian and the incompetent administrator.

KEEPING THE SYSTEM OPEN
AND MANAGEMENT FLEXIBLE

One of the keys to effective leadership in education is conflict resolution. Administrators must be sensitive to the interpersonal climate that exists in a college department or among the faculty members in a school. Particularly on most university campuses faculty rivalries and jealousies seem to prosper. Factions and cliques spring up. The interpersonal climate needs constant attention. Matters causing conflict and ill will must be brought out into the open for free discussion and resolution. An MBO system will set the stage for this vital interchange and discussion that must occur constantly if damaging conflicts are to be resolved.

The administrator must insist upon free and open discussion of problems that have their roots in personality difficulties. Different factions on a faculty should be openly recognized and the causes of the factionalism should be placed on the table. This will happen only if the administrator insists upon it and sets the tone for discussion that demands openness and candor.

In any organization the official power structure must reckon with the unofficial structure. The unofficial groups within a department or school create loyalties and generate causes that must be openly recognized and the circumstances surrounding them should be discussed by all concerned. Administrators should approach this in a nondefensive manner. Accusations should not be made but the fact of the existence of such unofficial groups should be recognized as part of the philosophy of administrative openness and candor.

Trust and confidence are usually products of a continuous process of free discussion in a nondefensive and nonaccusing atmosphere. It takes creative leadership and administrative candor to resolve conflicts and to keep factions from interfering with performance effectiveness. Too many conflicts are ignored and far too many issues that have overtones of unpleasantness are swept under the rug because administrators do not want to face the pain and stress. Particularly if the administrator is party to a conflict situation or if his actions may have resulted in certain interpersonal difficulties should the leader take the initiative in getting the wholesome therapy of free and open discussions started. This can usually take place without forcing someone to accept defeat or to become embarrassed and defensive. It all depends upon the skill of the leader in bringing out and helping those involved to face up to the issues and to express their feelings freely. By expressing good will and by showing a genuine determination to be helpful the school leader can approach his task as conflict resolver in an atmosphere that will be as nonthreatening as possible.

In resolving conflict and building sound interpersonal relationships we find the key to success in attaining teamwork, high morale, and readiness to give and take on issues. This starts with leadership example from the administrator. He must concede his mistakes and bring some humor into recognizing his weaknesses and imperfections. In this climate created by the leader the openness for reaching into the depths of other damaging interpersonal situations will come. Instead of smoothing over bad and undesirable interpersonal situations the administrator will, through his exemplary behavior, bring into the open for full discussion the situations that are dividing and impeding progress.

The foregoing discussion of conflict resolution should not imply that all interpersonal difficulties will be solved by merely being open and discussing them freely. Many problems and grievances have root causes that must be eradicated. Injustices certainly need to be corrected and genuine grievances need more than discussion for solution. But the first step to all of this is administrative candor on the part of those holding leadership responsibility. Freedom to give and take with the staff and constant readiness to candidly discuss problems must be part of the leadership style of the administrator. Particularly under a management system that is performance oriented is it necessary for all involved to have access to addressing the issues that tend to divide and factionalize an organization. Education, and particularly higher education, has not been free of the difficulties attendant upon unresolved conflicts and deep interpersonal difficulties. In addition to concentrating on the objectives and to moving the organization to accomplish the action steps committed under MBO, the administrator must be cognizant of the fact that he has to concentrate on the interpersonal circumstances in his organization and that the key to getting the total job done will rest in large part upon his human relations skills and his abilities as a conflict resolver and interpersonal problem mediator.

In discussing the potential of MBO to help reduce infighting and feuding on the campus, it should not be implied that all rivalries will cease and that there will be no more squabbles. This certainly will not happen. But MBO forces communication. It compels facing up to issues. The author has found the management review conferences (described in Chapter 6) to be particularly useful in getting issues out in the open. This clears the air and *tends to* keep the interpersonal climate healthy.

The therapy of talking things out is provided in MBO programs. The system, as a facilitator of discussion of real gut-level issues, has helped to keep key personalities fighting the problems rather than each other.

SUGGESTED TECHNIQUES IN GAINING STAFF INVOLVEMENT

The following are some suggestions for gaining staff involvement and commitment to reaching organizational objectives by sharing management responsibility:

(1) *Be sure to delegate.* The wise administrator does all that he can to establish conditions that will enhance probabilities for success. He permits his staff to grow by giving responsibility and delegating authority. Much of the detail as to how a certain outcome is to be attained should be left to the staff member to whom the responsibility has been delegated. We grow from the loads that we carry and from the pressure that we put upon ourselves as a result of decisions that we make.

(2) *Keep decision making as close as possible to the scene of the action.* This fundamental rule of administration is particularly important in MBO operations. Decision making is delegated downward, and top level management will find commitment and involvement emerging in ratio and proportion to the extent that the front office is successful in maximizing grass-roots level decision making.

(3) *Don't meddle.* Staff commitment to the goals of the organization will decline if administrators indulge in the damaging luxury of "suggesting" specific details that rightfully belong on a lower operational level. There is a distinct difference between emphasizing a keen interest and high expectation for results and entering into the details of dictating how the results might best be obtained at the

operational level. MBO makes it unnecessary for top management to get deeply involved in middle management affairs. Responsibilities are fixed and expectations are well understood.

(4) *Keep the rule book skinny.* A large and elaborate administrative code is not necessary where MBO is used. A few simple rules that will keep the organization operating within the law and within a few reasonable standardized procedures will be all that should be necessary. Creativity goes down when the rule book gets fat. A professional staff needs to operate in a climate conducive to inventiveness. Top management can, through management review conferences and continuous monitoring of results, keep a finger on operations and exercise strong leadership with less rule making and fewer policy directives in a situation where MBO charts the course and time-phased action steps developed by the staff spell out how to reach the ends that are sought. Thus, wise management focuses its attention upon ends and leaves the means to be developed within the framework of a few simple rules that express by their brevity full confidence in the professional staff.

(5) *Freely express recognition for good performance.* Through personal notes of congratulations and through telephone calls and informal visits, top management should constantly express recognition and congratulations for good performance. Insincere and trivial flattery is not, of course, useful or effective. What is needed are expressions of thanks and awareness when a fine piece of work has been completed by an individual or by a group belonging to the total team. This is often neglected by administrators. A short note, memo, or phone call takes only a few moments. The staff needs to know that there is interest and full cognizance of progress. Moreover, staff members need to know that the administration is aware of those responsible for unusual accomplishment.

(6) *Involve staff members in discussion before making decisions that will affect them.* Changes in procedures, allo-

cations of resources, priorities, and objectives should be made only after staff members have had ample time to discuss the implications for such decisions and have had an opportunity to react and make suggestions. MBO provides an ideal format for full participation in management decisions. Staff members will continue to feel membership and allegiance to the organizational team to the extent that they have opportunities to share in problems and to make contributions toward proposed solutions. This applies not only to the operational planning and objective-setting procedures described in earlier chapters. It is equally important to keep staff participation and involvement as the organization copes with unanticipated developments and changes that take place throughout the academic year. There is a distinct difference between having the staff members vote on every single decision and having them participate in the deliberations and discussions leading up to a decision. Weak and indecisive administration is typified by the practice of faculty meeting votes on every single difficult decision that has to be made. On the other hand, dictatorial and highhanded administration is characterized by a lack of discussion and failure to seek reaction and criticism to proposed changes in the operational practices and procedures of the organization. Discussion prior to decision making keeps before management a broader range of alternatives and a deeper quality of constructive criticism.

(7) *Anticipate action-forcing events so that ample time will be available for weighing alternatives.* Many arbitrary decisions are made by administrators because of failure on the part of the administrative staff to recognize early enough that a crucial decision will have to be made by a particular time certain. Many so-called crises became such because of management's failure to project ahead and anticipate in advance that certain things had to be done and certain issues had to be resolved within a specified time frame. Staff confidence in leadership at the top can

be badly shaken by obvious blunders in timing and placing in time perspective the action-forcing events that descend upon the institution. A management calendar will help to avoid hasty and seemingly arbitrary and dictatorial decisions.

ACADEMIC FREEDOM AND
PERFORMANCE RESPONSIBILITIES

A system of performance accountability as advocated in this book must recognize the values of academic freedom. Public school teachers and college professors must be allowed the freedom to do effective work in the classroom in a manner that reflects the best traditions of our democratic society. Teachers must be allowed latitude in working out specific details that will result in classroom performance that contributes to the organization's objectives. Teachers need to be free to probe, to raise questions, and to express and transmit truth to students as they know it. If students are to develop questioning and analytical minds it must follow that teachers should have the freedom to teach in a manner that will produce individual intellects with these qualities.

Performance responsibilities must be fixed with full cognizance of the foregoing statements about academic freedom. Needless to say, academic freedom does not confer upon teachers and professors unrestricted license to do as they please or perform without responsibility for results. If the administration is to be successful in MBO, policy should not be constructed in any way that will intimidate, distract, and put undue pressure on the orderly teaching-learning process. The special obligation upon the teacher to perform responsibly and to show results calls for a reciprocal recognition by administrators that there is a proper balance between rights and responsibilities in the area of academic freedom. MBO practices that gain staff involvement and participation in setting goals and formulating plans for attaining the same will result in the desired performance accountability advocated by the MBO system within a framework that recognizes that academic freedom in teaching is fundamental. Performance accountability and freedom to perform must go hand in hand.

Students and the public are free to judge the quality of a school or a department in a college or university. The entire system exists to serve the educational needs of the community. The accuracy and discipline in attaining performance accountability through MBO will make it possible for every professional staff member to answer more definitely the questions of quality and quantity of performance raised by students and the public in general. As the professional staff learns that MBO will provide quick and relevant answers to criticism, they will, the author believes, become more fully committed to this system of management. It provides insurance against unwarranted and unjustified attack and criticism. This is no small matter in these days of pressure tactics and groundless incriminations.

SUMMARY

This chapter has emphasized democratic procedures, staff involvement in decision making, techniques for delegating responsibility, the need for emphasizing results and de-emphasizing rules and red tape. The need for administrators to be cognizant of the pressures and apprehensions that can be generated by a performance accountability system has been pointed out. Considerable space has been devoted to discussing the rights as well as the performance responsibilities of teachers and professors. By setting out the conditions that will make success more probable and by deliberately avoiding decision making at upper levels when it can be appropriately made on the grass-roots level, the administrator keeps the responsibility where it belongs and leaves the means in the hands of the staff while looking at the ends by expressing interest in results and freely recognizing and offering congratulations for outstanding performance.

8

Getting an MBO System Started

The problems of initiating an MBO system will be discussed in this chapter. Some specific do's and don'ts are emphasized, and anticipated staff frustrations and advice on how to meet them are covered.

LEARNING BY DOING

Like most new ventures to be implemented in a complex organization, MBO should be assimilated gradually into the school system or university management framework. The best approach, the author believes, is to move into some limited aspects of MBO after a very brief and simple orientation and explanation have been completed. One learns to utilize a management system more by actual experience than by studying abstract theories and concepts.

Training should run concurrently with experience. Staff members will be more interested in the fundamental principles of MBO if they are concurrently confronted with the task of implementing a limited aspect of the system into the organization. As actual experience makes its impact the learner will have immediate reason for the information. Because of this need, the concepts will not be so obscure and hard to grasp. Stated simply but tritely, the best way to begin is to begin.

This is not to say that a large and complex educational organization should leap blindly into implementing a management system. MBO can be phased into gradually by taking a few simple steps, by adapting and managing to accomplish one or two easy-to-attain objectives. Concurrent with doing this some fundamental ideas can be taught. By getting results orientation into the system and results consciousness among the staff through some rudimentary efforts, openness can be created for training and further progress.

The author successfully implemented a rudimentary form of MBO in a large school system with a student population of over sixty thousand. All seventy-two of the schools in this system started at the same time. The schools adopted and managed to accomplish a number of significant objectives with the first efforts occurring after the school year was well under way. This satisfactory but far from perfect beginning was under way after two orientation sessions with the top central office staff and after only one orientation session with the principals of the school system.

A simple two-page sheet of instructions accompanied by the superintendent's performance priorities and some MBO system forms were placed in the hands of the principals. It was explained that the effort would be a learning experience and that only a limited number of objectives should be adopted by each school for management to accomplishment as the members of the administrative team learned what MBO was all about.

All the schools were urged to adopt their own objectives, but they were also cautioned to give careful consideration to the district-wide performance priorities. It was emphasized that during the practice and learning endeavor the administrative staff would share experiences and learn together as the principles of MBO were discussed and applied in a practical situation.

ANTICIPATE FRUSTRATION

As a staff of busy administrators attain first exposure to the idea of management by objectives a typical response will be that the entire effort is a "bunch of Mickey Mouse busywork." This was the author's first impression of MBO. Until administrators grasp the full value and understand the real need for operating under a management system, there will be an element of frustration and resentment. Experienced school leaders feel that they already know how to manage their units. They feel that they are doing fairly well and they see no need for facing the changes demanded by MBO.

This reaction, the author believes, will be less prolonged if the administrative staff gets some immediate hands on experience. Inservice training prior to activity in placing MBO in operation places added demands on busy administrators. Moreover, they will not see the need for these demands and for the detailed work of MBO if they spend time studying without having the opportunity to immediately apply the system to the problems they know exist in their schools. Some frustration and negative reaction will be inevitable regardless of how the management system is implemented. The duration and intensity of these reactions will be reduced if training and actual application run concurrently.

Many administrators are needlessly frustrated in their initial experiences because MBO is described in a manner that gives the impression of extensive detail and complexity. Its simplicity and usefulness are obscured by instructional rhetoric in the inservice classrooms.

It must be conceded that full and ultimate use of a management system to attain performance accountability throughout a large and complex university or school system requires a journey of several years. But if this is pointed out with great emphasis to an administrative staff in a series of inservice training sessions where complex planning networks are presented and extensive evaluations are described in all their threatening detail, the very thought of the amount of work and study involved will add to the problems of gaining acceptance and support. Gradual application is preferred to this approach. Let the skills grow gradually and in the due course of time.

Leaders responsible for getting MBO started should play down the complexities and emphasize the simplicity and ease of using the system in its most rudimentary form. Successful experience is contagious. Success begets more success and calls for a step that will lead to more sophistication. When a new system begins to attain results it sells itself to the top leaders. This will be particularly true in educational organizations that have been operating without any formalized system of management.

By utilizing the forms and simple explanations found in Appendix D the author successfully gained early commitment to MBO and was able to cut down on the period of negative response. An expert sophisticated in network planning, in systems analysis, and in the use of highly complex evaluative techniques will surely scorn the simplified explanation and the skimpy instructions represented by the sample papers found in Appendix D. But by getting the administrative staff to jump quickly into the reality of using at least a crude model of a management system, the interest and commitment become self-generating as an inherent part of learning by doing. The need for deeper study becomes apparent, and the front office is in the nice position of responding to demand rather than forcing and pushing MBO in full-bloom form from the outset.

The critical time in implementing a management system is that period in the total experience where administrators come to realize that their daily operations have not been guided by a plan and by a system that is results oriented, and that focuses the efforts of the entire staff on the same targets that have been accepted by all as the priority problems to be solved. As the administrator begins to see how MBO can function to solve some of his most pressing problems he will also see that his institution needs a management system. He will begin to use the system to direct his staff members so that there will be better teamwork and so that outcomes will be well defined and responsibilities fully understood. At this point he will become an advocate of MBO. But until this happens, he will be a skeptic at best and possibly a very negative opponent at worst.

KEEPING THE LOAD LIGHT
DURING ORIENTATION

A key point to be considered in starting an MBO system is to minimize technicalities and to persuade with simplicity and a light touch. The entire system's management habits cannot be changed in one fell swoop. The first efforts will be crude and less than fully productive. But the main purpose should be to move gradually from a system of marginal performance accountability to a point where substantial results orientation is attained. If criticism is spared and the impulse to jump to a program in full bloom the first year is resisted, more progress will be made in the long run.

Some school units or college departments will prepare objectives that are far from being finite and measurable. If the objectives are poorly written and the time-phased steps for reaching them are fuzzy the front office should be patient and look for teaching moments. The perfectionist who insists on the first effort being precise and technically correct will add to the problems of gaining commitment. The system itself will teach administrators. Being intelligent people, they will seek the higher levels of performance once they see how the system works and how they can use it as a useful tool.

The initial experience in the MBO system should be to begin with a few objectives. Possibly three objectives should be a maximum the first year. At the outside, not more than five should be permitted. It must be kept in mind that the school or department has its regular load to carry. The special effort required calls for a limited number of simple-to-manage objectives so that the load is kept light and the attitudes are positive.

It will be wise not to outline all the details of each of the steps in the MBO cycle for a full academic year as the institution takes its first faltering steps in attaining performance accountability through use of a management system. The staff should be led one step at a time through the process so that complexities are not emphasized too early in the game.

WRITTEN GUIDELINES FOR
BEGINNERS IN MBO

In making preparations to initiate an MBO system a simple handbook containing basic information will be useful. This handbook should contain the following information:

1. A brief and concise statement about MBO and how the management system will help the institution to attain performance accountability through orientation of the staff toward results. This statement should be void of technical terminology.
2. Samples of objectives that are good examples for beginners. These should deal with subject matter of current concern to the institution. Complex examples requiring sub-objectives should be avoided.

The sample objectives found in Appendix B represent the type of simple, straightforward statements that describe performance commitments. Examples such as these will be helpful in the written guidelines.

3. Descriptive information about the performance priorities of the institution or school system.
4. Examples of time-phased action steps that show how operational planning will execute the management of an objective to accomplishment.
5. The simple outline steps in an annual MBO cycle, showing suggested dates when certain events occur. The MBO cycle information should not break out all the detail known to exist in the plans of a mature system that has been in operation for a number of years.
6. A very brief statement of the duties of various principal officers in the organization. Care must be taken not to portray a long and difficult task.

7. The simple reporting forms necessary to support the efforts of the first year. The forms should be as self-explanatory as possible, with a minimum of written instructions.

SUMMARY

It should be encouraging to school and college executives to note that a large and complex organization such as the U. S. Department of Health, Education and Welfare has implemented an MBO system. HEW has over 110,000 employees. Unlike the federal government, HEW prepared a very brief and simple handbook with the information recommended in this chapter. The author was Acting U.S. Commissioner of Education and Deputy Commissioner during the early months of this effort. From this experience, the author became convinced that educational organizations could implement the operation of MBO with less effort and travail than that experienced by the staff of HEW.

The key to successful implementation of MBO is a simple beginning. The expectation at the outset should be frustration. Experience and training should run concurrently during the initial weeks. Technical language and complex training, planning, and evaluating systems should be avoided. The present burdens on staff members should be taken into account as MBO is implemented.

The school system beginning with no previous experience in MBO should start with a very simple and easy needs assessment effort. Concurrent with the needs assessment effort, the staff should receive some orientation, following the guidelines described earlier in this chapter. Practice in writing objectives should be given. The examples contained in Appendix B are very simple and should be easy to use as models for beginners.

For the beginning staff, the performance priorities should be few. They should avoid ambiguity and complexity. In getting an MBO system started, it is wise to avoid tackling difficult and complex problems until some experience is gained with simple, easy-to-attain objectives.

The chief executive and his staff should allow objectives to be accepted as performance commitments if they have the enthusiastic support of the faculty. It is more important to have this enthusiasm than it is to have precision and accuracy. Many MBO initiatives fail because of heavy demands that discourage the staff and because of the imposition of objectives that do not have the commitment and enthusiasm of the faculty.

The following story illustrates the need for keeping the MBO task within reach of the staff: A man hired by a psychologist was asked to do some work under special experimental circum-stances. He was given an ax and was told to pretend that he was chopping wood. He was offered five times the going wage rate for such work, but was instructed to use the back side of the ax. The man accepted. He thought the psychologist was foolish to pay such a price for getting nothing done. Since the wages were very high, he did not mind, so he went to work.

In two hours the man knocked at the psychologist's door to announce that he was quitting. When asked why he was quitting, the ax man replied: "I'm quitting this job. The pay is good, but when I chop wood I've got to see the chips fly."

We all must gain satisfaction from our work. We must feel that we are accomplishing something. A sense of progress and momentum is important. Particularly in the beginning months of MBO, the task must be made easy and the effort rewarding to the staff.

To convey to the reader how MBO can be started without use of complex technical terminology and elaborate preparation and training, the example on the following pages is presented. This example is an actual sample MBO plan developed in a small elementary school. The staff completed this effort with very little training and with no outside assistance. Note the perfor-mance accountability that has been developed to commit this school to results-oriented action to solve the problem described. This type of MBO effort does not require elaborate planning net-works using PERT and other complex systems analysis efforts. It is easy to implement this level of MBO work. With only a few hours of orientation and training, effective MBO efforts such as this can be started.

SUBJECT:

Math Skills

SCHOOL:

Plymouth

PROBLEM DESCRIPTION:

All Seventh Grade students entering the junior high schools of Granite School District were administered a district made diagnostic test in mathematics at the beginning of this school year. The test results seemed to indicate that much of the failure students were experiencing in mathematics was due to failure to master the basic arithmetic facts at specified times in the elementary school. Plymouth School is a feeder school to a junior high school that tested below the district norm in this test. This would seem to generally indicate that this problem might be more serious at Plymouth School than in the average school in the district. Evidence would certainly indicate a need for immediate action to be taken to correct this deficiency.

STATEMENT OF MAJOR OBJECTIVE:

It has been established as a major objective for the Plymouth School to teach the basic addition, subtraction, multiplication and division facts and achieve a level of mastery in terms of preset standards for each grade level. This objective will be accomplished between Monday, September 18, 1972, when the program will be initiated and Friday, May 18, 1973, when the program will have been concluded.

STATEMENT OF SUB-OBJECTIVE:

1. By May 18, 1973, 90% of the kindergarten children will be able to identify and recognize the number numeral concepts 0-10, learn to count and write from 1-10 and perform the operation of addition to sums of 5 with 95% accuracy.

2. By May 18, 1973, 85% of the First Grade students will have mastered with 95% accuracy the 100 basic addition and subtraction facts for instant recall when administered in a 6 and 7 minute timed written test.

3. By May 18, 1973, 90% of the Second Grade students will have mastered with 95% accuracy the 100 basic addition and subtraction facts for instant recall when administered in a 5½ to 6 minute timed written test. Eighty five percent of the Second Grade students will have mastered with 95% accuracy the basic multiplication facts for instant recall as follows when administered in a 4 minute timed written test:

    > 0 times table through 9 times
    > 1 times table through 9 times
    > 2 times table through 9 times
    > 3 times table through 9 times
    > 4 times table through 5 times
    > 5 times table through 5 times

4. By May 18, 1973, 93% of the Third Grade students will have mastered with 95% accuracy the 100 basic addition and subtraction facts for instant recall when administered in a four minute timed written test. Eighty-five percent of the Third Grade students will have mastered with 95% accuracy the basic multiplication facts up through 9 x 9 and the basic division facts up through 9 ÷ 81 when administered in a five minute timed written test.

5. By May 18, 1973, 93% of the Fourth Grade students will have mastered with 95% accuracy the 100 basic addition and subtraction facts for instant recall when administered in a 3½ minute timed written test. Eighty-five percent of the Fourth Grade students will have mastered with 95% accuracy the basic multiplication facts up through 12 x 12 and the basic division facts up through 12 ÷ 144 for instant recall when administered in a five minute timed written test.

MBO FORM B - Time Phased Action Steps to Attain Major Objectives or Significant Sub-Objectives (to be used to monitor progress in MBO)

Name of School   PLYMOUTH   59

Administrative Complex   CENTRAL

Principal   A. Leon Tobler

In the form below list the detailed action steps to be executed in accomplishing the objective or sub-objective. The following symbols will denote beginning dates and completion dates for each action step:

○ = month and day action step is initiated

△ = month and day action step is completed

——— = the line shows the duration of activity from initiation to completion

Projected Completion Date	Action Steps	Staff Member Responsible	MONTHS												Explanation & Detail on Page No.
			J	A	S	O	N	D	J	F	M	A	M	J	
9-12-72	Principal will review with teachers stated objectives and testing procedures	A. Leon Tobler			○12										
9-15-72	Prepare testing and reporting forms	A. Leon Tobler		○1	△15										
9-18-72	Pre-tests will be administered	All teachers			△18										
10-3-72	General review of methods for teaching Math skills. Teachers will prepare plans	A. Leon Tobler / All teachers			○30 / 25										
5-18-73	Biweekly tests will be given and monitored	All teachers / A. Leon Tobler			○29								△18		
11-14-72	Parents will be contacted by teachers and help and support solicited	All teachers			△18	△14							△18		
11-21-72	Quarterly review with teachers and teacher's plans for next quarter	A. Leon Tobler / All teachers				○13									
1-30-73	Quarterly review with teachers and teacher's plans for next quarter	A. Leon Tobler / All teachers							△22						
3-7-73	Parents will be contacted by teachers for the second time and help and support solicited	All teachers									△7				
4-3-73	Quarterly review with teachers and teacher's plan for next quarter	A. Leon Tobler / All teachers										△6			

C-2460-4 (Rev. 1-7-72)

Page No. 59

MBO FORM B - Time Phased Action Steps to Attain Major Objectives or Significant
Sub-Objectives (to be used to monitor progress in MBO)

Name of School   PLYMOUTH   60

Administrative Complex   CENTRAL

Principal   A. Leon Tobler

In the form below list the detailed action steps to be executed in accomplishing the objective or sub-objective. The following symbols will denote beginning dates and completion dates for each action step

◯ = month and day action step is initiated

△ = month and day action step is completed

——— = the line shows the duration of activity from initiation to completion

Projected Completion Date	Action Steps	Staff Member Responsible	MONTHS												Explanation & Detail on Page No.
			J	A	S	O	N	D	J	F	M	A	M	J	
5-18-73	Teachers will administer post tests and report results	All teachers											① △18		
5-22-73	Conduct evaluation of goal effectiveness	A. Leon Tobler											△22		

C-2460-4 (Rev. 1-7-72)

Page No.   60

Detailed Explanation of Action Step and How the Same Will be Accomplished

Action Step No. 1

On September 12, 1972, the principal will meet with all teachers
and conduct a review of the stated objectives and the action steps for
achieving these objectives. Plans for administering the pretests will
be outlined.

Action Step No. 2

By September 15, 1972, the office staff will have prepared all the
testing forms to be used by all teachers in administering the pretests
and forms for reporting pupil progress to the principal biweekly.

Action Step No. 3

On Monday, September 18, 1972, all teachers will administer the
appropriate pretests to their students. All teachers will introduce the
skills and objectives of this MBO to their students in such a way as to
stress the urgency for success in mastering the skills.

Action Step No. 4

On Tuesday, September 25, 1972, the principal will meet with all
teachers and conduct a general review of methods for teaching the math
skills involved. The methods reviewed will be those prepared by staff
planning committees the year before while working on this MBO. All teachers
will be assigned to select their methods and prepare a written plan for
teaching the skills involved during the first quarter of the school year.
These plans will be submitted to the principal on or before the next staff
meeting scheduled for Tuesday, October 3.

Action Step No. 5

Beginning Friday, September 29, 1972, and continuing biweekly throughout the year, all teachers will administer an achievement test and report
the pupil progress to the principal on the appropriate form.

The principal will monitor the pupil progress reports. He will meet
with any teacher whose students are not making consistent progress. He will
explore with the teacher ways and means for correcting any deficiencies in the
program and give help where it seems necessary.

Action Step No. 6

On or before November 14, 1972, all teachers will have contacted the
parents of their students to solicit their help and support in teaching the
basic math facts to their respective child.

Action Step No. 7

During the week of November 13-17, 1972, the principal will conduct a
quarterly review with each teacher concerning their class progress in mastering the math skills involved. Each teacher will be asked to prepare an outline for teaching these math skills during the next quarter of the school year.

Action Step No. 8

During the week of January 22-26, 1973, the principal will conduct a quarterly review with each teacher concerning their class progress in mastering the math skills involved. Each teacher will be asked to prepare an outline for teaching these math skills during the next quarter of the school year. Teaching plans will be due on January 30, 1973.

Action Step No. 9

On or before March 7, 1973, all teachers will have contacted, for the second time during the school year, the parents of their students to solicit their help and support in teaching the basic math facts to their respective child.

Action Step No. 10

During the week of March 26-30, 1973, the principal, will conduct a quarterly review with each teacher concerning their class progress in mastering the math skills involved. Each teacher will be asked to prepare an outline for teaching these math skills during the next quarter of the school year. Teaching plans will be due on April 3, 1973.

Action Step No. 11

On May 18, 1973, all teachers will administer the respective post tests to their students and report the results to the principal.

Action Step No. 12

On May 22, 1973, the principal will meet with all teachers and conduct an evaluation of goal effectiveness. Each action step will be evaluated for its effectiveness in achieving the stated objectives.

9

The Role of the Chief
Executive in MBO

In this chapter the crucial responsibilities of the chief executive officer will be discussed. The use of MBO as a management tool in the hands of the college president or superintendent of schools will be outlined in some detail. The responsibility of the chief executive officer to keep a proper balance between autocratic and laissez-faire leadership will be described. More detail on the role of the chief executive officer in conducting management review conferences with heads of major units in his organization will be covered. The need for the chief executive to pay particular attention to his responsibility in establishing conditions that will increase probabilities for success will be emphasized. And finally, the leadership charisma and style of the chief executive officer in utilizing MBO will comprise the concluding paragraphs.

LEARNING TO USE MBO AS
A MANAGEMENT TOOL

The chief executive officer should learn to utilize MBO as a powerful tool to guide his institution, coordinate the efforts of staff members, and direct the institutional energies in a very deliberate and predetermined direction. He has in his hands a system that has power to drive and steer the institution where he wants it to go. MBO is to the chief executive what a steering wheel is to an automobile if he utilizes it skillfully to gain maximum efficiency in directing and managing the resources at his command.

The priority-setting and problem-solving potential of this management system must be thoroughly understood by the chief executive officer. The dynamics of management are different because the system sets up action-forcing events within certain time frames. This begets momentum for special efforts to attack high priority problems. The chief executive, as he thinks and acts in terms of the objectives in the system, can keep his institution alive with interest in the progress that was preconceived in operational planning and is executed throughout the course of an entire academic year. This progress is noted by the quantification of results. Interest in a steady flow of progress data will be manifested throughout the organization if the chief executive constantly refers to the information emanating from the special project efforts of MBO. In this sense, the chief executive sets the tone for keeping the system from becoming stagnant. His problem-solving orientation and his results-oriented management efforts will help everyone to use MBO as a management tool.

If, on the other hand, the chief executive officer relates to the MBO system as something aside from the mainstream of his managing and directing efforts, MBO will not function as a management system and realize the potential that it has for facilitating effective and dynamic leadership.

The chief executive must, in analyzing his role and responsibility, leave sufficient latitude for his unit heads to develop special projects of particular interest to them. As he uses MBO to drive and direct the total institution, his priorities on the lower levels will not receive attention. This will require some insight and empathy on the part of the chief executive to keep the front office from being too heavy-handed and, at the same time, retain a heavy enough touch to get done what has to be accomplished to reach his priorities and purposes.

As the chief executive uses MBO as a management tool, his leadership behavior must be such that others can also claim it for their purposes. It is a system-wide management program and the wise executive will also leave room for others to offer initiatives through the system.

ESTABLISHING CONDITIONS THAT WILL ENHANCE PROBABILITIES FOR SUCCESS

The chief executive officer should use MBO to encourage creativity and not stifle it. When he approves the objectives and the operational plan of a unit head he must be prepared to follow up with the necessary support that can come only from his office. Dollar and staff resources will have to be allocated in full cognizance of the objectives that have been set. This will require some priority decisions from the front office in eliminating lower priority claims on dollars and staff. This, needless to say, will be difficult and will generate some conflict.

The top executive must be ready to call the shots and face up to the difficult decisions. The amount of decisiveness and management courage displayed by him will convey to others in the institution the degree of his serious commitment to MBO as a mode of operation. Since this management system forces priority setting and resource allocating on the basis of priorities there must be readiness and total willingness to make decisions and take the heat from them on the part of the chief executive officer. He must be sensitive to the fact that objectives will be reached only if he establishes the conditions that are requisites for success.

MANAGEMENT REVIEW CONFERENCES WITH HEADS OF MAJOR UNITS

A prior chapter discussed the need for management review conferences and made some references to the role of the chief executive officer in these conferences. In putting emphasis on the unique and special responsibilities of the chief executive officer in MBO it is important to stress the fact that this key function should be carried out only by the top executive.

The chief executive officer should hold management review conferences with the heads of major units who have made performance commitments under the MBO system. These conferences should be held at least once each month and more often when necessary. In the author's experience with this type of management system it was found that the time pressures on the chief executive often resulted in neglect of management review conferences. Many times such conferences have been postponed several times each month or delegated to a subordinate officer. Both practices lead to problems. If the chief executive officer wants to manage his organization with this management system he must be prepared to make the personal time commitments necessary for success. In no instance will these time commitments be more crucial than in the matter of holding regular and timely management review conferences.

Since some of the details of the conference have been treated elsewhere some of the important indirect outcomes will be discussed here. No matter how carefully the operational planning is executed, unanticipated developments will necessitate changes in management strategy and reallocation of resources from time to time during the academic year. The management review conference provides a forum where the heads of major units can discuss problems and describe unanticipated developments that ought to be called to the attention of the chief executive. New channels of communication and deeper mutual understanding and respect should emerge from these regularly held conferences with the chief executive officer.

The management review conference provides an opportunity for the chief executive to sit down with a unit head and frankly discuss his stewardship over his part of the institution. It is a reporting session wherein performance accountability is the prime subject matter. The role of the chief executive officer in these conferences must be to convey a concern and an expectation that the performance commitments made when objectives were adopted will be accomplished. This, however, should be expressed in a non-threatening and supportive atmosphere. The conduct of the chief executive should be such that full candor will result. Both the chief executive and his unit head must be willing to chew on the problems and not on each other. If the conversation is kept in the direction of results and facts, with personalities coming in only when necessary and germane to the results orientation, then the outcome will be productive. If certain results are disappointing and below what can reasonably be expected, the top executive should lend encouragement at the same time that he conveys in a firm but kindly way that he will be looking for some progress and possible reversal of the trend the following month when he sits across the table from his unit head to get another accounting of his stewardship. The unit head should leave the conference feeling that he has the support and confidence of his boss. He should also leave the conference feeling that his strengths and outstanding accomplishments were recognized and appropriate praise was given. And finally, he should leave the conference with a positive feeling that certain levels of performance must be upgraded and certain milestone events of accomplishment will be expected when the next conference is held.

It is particularly important that the chief executive behave in a manner that will make it possible for subordinates to inform him of malfunctions and problems generated by his office. The identification of deficiencies should be a two-way street. If this is not readily recognized by the unit head the chief executive may want to conclude the conference by inquiring about problems that may be caused by his immediate office. He may inquire about how his office may be of assistance and if there are problems requiring their joint initiatives in attaining solution.

Some aspects of the management review conference should be somewhat confidential. There will be times when only the chief executive and the unit head should be present. At other times, however, the management review conference should be used as a wider forum for discussion among key people in the organization about the problems and accomplishments of the unit under review. The chief executive should encourage the attendance of others as a means of enhancing communication, gaining commitment, and attaining personal relationships that are often missing in large organizations. If the conferences are conducted in a businesslike manner with a high premium placed upon the time spent, the chief executive should be able to attain the desired outcomes described above without excessive demands upon his time. Wise and frugal use of time during the management review conference will result in making it possible for such conferences to be held regularly.

The chief executive should prepare for each management review conference. His staff should brief him on developments and prepare him for critical issues. Above all, he must be informed and he must convey awareness and interest in the unit and its accomplishments. If he shows that he cares enough to keep up to date, the unit head and his subordinates will realize that their work is very important in the eyes of the top man. If a problem of particular concern has been solved or if considerable progress has been made towards its solution since the last management review conference the chief executive might well begin with enthusiastic acclaim for the outstanding performance. If he can find reason to begin on a positive note, dig in hard on the problems, and then conclude in a positive and supportive tone at the end of the conference a constructive and productive attitude is likely to prevail. The chief executive must keep in mind that he cannot afford to indulge in "chewing out" his subordinates when he is disappointed in performance if such action will not be productive and result in the desired outcomes. Too often many of us act on emotion and respond emotionally. The management review conference should be free from this. The chief executive should approach the conference thinking about motivation, reinforcement of desired outcomes, building morale, and emphasizing those points that will lead to a resolve to attain the highest level of excellence. His leadership personality will be on display and he needs to keep in mind that the unit and his staff will hold a post-mortem on the conference where what he says and how he behaves will be topics of discussion. His credibility and particularly the level of confidence in his leadership will increase or decrease at each of these management review conferences.

KEEPING SPAN OF CONTROL
WITHIN REACH

A very significant side benefit of management review conferences with heads of major units is the fact that the chief executive officer must analyze how he can relate effectively to those persons and to those units that report directly to him. If the chief executive cannot find time to meet with all the unit heads in management review conferences it might be that his span of control is too wide. He may have entirely too many persons and too many units reporting directly to him. Very often a chief executive who says that he cannot find time to meet with unit heads reporting to him in management review conference sessions is actually saying that he has a wider span of responsibility and control than he can manage. The MBO system focuses upon this and should lead the chief executive to be more introspective about his own confidence in relating to those key persons who must receive instruction, direction, and support from his immediate office. Very often the installation of a management system such as MBO results in reorganization. Such reorganization cleans up lines of responsibility and channels of communication. Awareness of the necessity for this usually comes out of the management review conferences.

KEEPING A PROPER BALANCE BETWEEN
AUTOCRATIC AND LAISSEZ-FAIRE LEADERSHIP

Because of the nature of educational organizations, considerable emphasis has been given in this book to the concept of democratic decision making, participatory management, and showing deference and respect for professional colleagues in the leadership behavior of administrators. The hard line and somewhat ruthless use of management systems in industry to attain greater production or higher volume sales cannot be successfully duplicated in public schools and colleges. What can be duplicated, however, is the results orientation of industry. Management practices and particularly management preoccupation with profits is replaced by education's concern for serving the needs of the student body and generally upgrading the human potential of the society served. This can be more efficiently done with a management system guiding the efforts and coordinating the teamwork potentialities of large educational establishments.

Many aspects of the educational enterprise have not been subjected to the discipline of performance accountability that comes from a very hard and firm commitment to objectives and from results orientation. The chief executive officer should use MBO to attain this desirable and badly needed intensity on the part of the staff toward results. He should seek through the system creative and positive tension without resorting to heavy-handed and oppressive pressure.

The increasing demand of professionals — teachers in public schools and professors on college campuses — to have a hand in management and to be consulted on decisions that affect them can find some substantive reconciliation in a management system such as MBO. What is more, the chief executive can use the system to satisfy this understandable demand on the one hand and to avoid a laissez-faire and goal-less operation on the other. Many administrators in education complain that participatory management and introduction of many democratic decision-making procedures will result in performance flabbiness and slothfulness in results. In the author's experience, this need not be so if the chief executive uses his management system with the skill and insight that will strike this balance properly between autocratic and laissez-faire leadership.

In the leadership behavior of the chief executive must be found this willingness to share and to involve professionals in the management of the school system or the university. Without this the modern educational administrator fails. But with the management system, performance expectations will not decline but will be enhanced. The dialogue and participation permit the elements of democracy to prevail but the performance commitments and results-quantified objectives keep the badly needed elements of firmness and performance discipline before the entire staff. MBO, if wisely used by the chief executive officer, will provide a system that will permit the staff to largely manage themselves. What is expected and what is attained is fully in the open and on display. From this staff members can help each other and bring certain elements of creative pressure upon the few laggards found in any institution. Such openness and peer group pressure applies, of course, to administrators as well as to professors and teachers.

The chief executive officer should welcome the institution-wide performance introspection that comes from MBO. He should see that the system in his institution is designed in a way that enhances democratic procedures in decision making and maximizes dialogue and participatory management. His leadership in the MBO program should strike a proper balance between dictatorial and autocratic methods on the one hand and abdication of leadership resulting in performance slothfulness on the other.

CHARISMA AND STYLE OF THE CHIEF EXECUTIVE

The chief executive must display certain leadership qualities that relate to his intellectual power, wit, charm, magnetism, and general strength of character. In brief, if he is to become a truly exceptional executive he must have charisma. Theologically speaking charisma is described as a power bestowed by God. This, of course, is overstating the matter. But the aggregate of the qualities of the mind, personality, and character of the executive must be such that he is recognized and respected as a leader. He must have the capacity to earn respect through his performance and through the influence of his personal powers in relating to his staff and to others. If he is to be a truly great educational leader he must have magnetism and display those qualities that attract and command respect. His use of power and authority, his intellect, sense of humor, capacity to communicate and persuade, and the overall magnetism bound up in his total person must give him those qualities of administrative leadership charisma that will draw the staff, the governing board, the student body, and the public in general to respect and give thoughtful but positive response to his initiatives as he guides and directs the affairs of the university or school system.

As a public figure the school executive has both legal and charismatic authority and power. He has the legal power bestowed upon him by virtue of the office he holds. Initially, upon taking office, this gives him great power and influence over others. But the real power that will increase or decline after he has assumed office is his charismatic power. *This he must earn.* Through his performance and out of his leadership behavior and personality will emerge this true capacity for great leadership. His strength and steadiness under pressure, and his genuine commitment, undergirded by a bright mind and a sense of humor, will all contribute to his charisma. Some executives continue to expand the effectiveness and leadership power of their positions by virtue of outstanding leadership ability and continue commitment to increasingly high levels of performance. Others seem to move along on a level plateau or even experience a decline in influence and leadership power below that level inherited with the position on the day they assumed office.

Through use of a management system like MBO the chief executive officer has an unusually effective means of enhancing his own leadership capabilities and building his personal administrative charisma. This, of course, he will be seeking for the outcomes of the institution over which he has responsibility and only secondarily as a means of personal enhancement. Education is for the fulfillment of the potential of human beings in living their lives. The emphasis upon numbers and quantification of performance in this book can be justified only insofar as these factors have implications for improving the quality of living and the quality of service rendered to human beings. The effective chief executive officer will be cognizant of this and will conduct the affairs of his office with this point foremost in his mind. Sydney P. Marland once said, "As we pursue the practice of management by objectives, we must always remember the basic imperative of education: the eternal and transcending obligation to be humane. Our primary concern must always be the fulfillment of individual human beings rather than the fulfillment of managerial concepts.* Such should be the role of the chief executive officer as he uses his management system to attain performance accountability. The reform and renewal of his institution accomplished through MBO will reflect in large part his administrative philosophy, style and character.

As the chief executive officer uses MBO to improve his institution and to improve his own leadership effectiveness he must be very introspective about how he relates to others. His sensitivity should tell him that he should carry out his management activities in a way that will earn respect and increase his influence. The following are some critical check-list type items that have been emphasized in this book but that need additional emphasis in this chapter of analysis of the role and leadership style of the chief executive:

(1) *Strive for fair and equitable treatment of the staff.* Be constantly careful about showing favorites and favoritism.

(2) *Make competence and performance the key to promotion.* Make sure that the other administrators in the system follow this principle. It is easy to look to friends and close associates when a new appointment is about to be made. The emphasis upon objectivity and performance accountability should carry over into the matter of making promotions.

(3) *Make decisions when they are needed without undue delay.* Be sure that the decision is defensible and that there is a solid basis for it, and then act decisively.

(4) *Be consistent and do not vacillate.* Show your ability to make decisions in the face of pressure. Be sure you are right and then be firm. Leadership requires decisiveness. Vacillation and delay will destroy respect and erode leadership authority.

(5) *Delegate responsibility and support those to whom you delegate.* Let others make decisions. Enhance their decision-making capacity by giving the back-up and authority necessary for decision making. Be constantly cognizant of the decisions

*Message of U.S. Commissioner of Education to staff meeting of Office of Education in January of 1971.

that you make and constantly delegate to unit heads that authority and responsibility that will ultimately make the unit more
effective.

(6) *Be understood.* Say what you mean and mean what
you say. Be direct, avoid wordiness, and make sure that your
administrative pronouncements are unambiguous, concise, and
straight to the point.

(7) *Keep your word.* Do not overpromise. Don't "cry wolf."
When you express concern or anger over a matter make sure that
it is worthy of the emphasis it is getting. We are all just as small
as the things we will let bother us. The chief executive must concern himself about large matters and should not "cry wolf" about
small and inconsequential items not worthy of his stature or position. Commitments that are made must be kept. That is why it
is important to keep your word and avoid over-promising. If the
commitments of the chief executive are always matched by performance a fine precedent for the entire institution will exist.

(8) *Find time to show concern for misfortune, to commend
excellence, and to offer encouragement during stress and difficulty.* This thoughtfulness will go a long way toward building the
credibility and image of the chief executive officer. Too little
time is invested by the chief executive in offering encouragement
and commendation. The chief executive should make sure that
he takes the time to carry out this very important morale-build-
ing responsibility that is his and his alone.

(9) *Be warm, humane, and operate with the smallest possible ego.* Have a big heart and an open mind as you deal with
your colleagues.

(10) *Follow through and remember significant details.* Sort
out the significant from the less significant and keep your mind
filled only with the larger details and facts. Be sure to follow
through and to perform in such a manner that others will know
that you are going to follow through and check up on the conclusion or culmination of any substantive matter that occupies
your attention.

(11) *Admit your errors.* Admit them openly and forthright-

ly. Assume the full blame for your wrong decisions and don't take too much credit for the right ones.

(12) *When a big decision is coming up, hear all sides.* Be sure to hear the views that are opposite from your own. Weigh evidence carefully and let it be known throughout your organization that you will listen to others and hear all sides before making a decision.

The executives who lose the confidence of staff members are those who indulge in some of the following practices:

1. Have a "palace guard" that is close to the front office and that has first call on promotions and all inside information. In this circumstance the executive usually hears only what he wants to hear.
2. Make decisions only to change them when the heat is on. This lack of administrative courage stands out quickly.
3. Shift to others the blame for errors that obviously belong to the chief executive.
4. Delegate responsibility and then meddle in affairs, capriciously giving instructions when the impulse seems strong.
5. Permit and encourage staff members to go around unit heads in bringing matters to the front office.
6. Jump at conclusions without weighing evidence.
7. Pass the buck to the board or the administrative council when unpopular decisions have to be made.

FUTURE-ORIENTED LEADERSHIP

The effective school executive should use MBO to provide effective management now and future-oriented leadership that will be in contact with what is coming up in our society. It is trite but true to emphasize that we must be concerned about the future for that is where our students will be living. The future-orientation of MBO planning must be mellowed by a sense of history and by some feeling of the past and its relationship to now and to the future.

Coping with change and shaping change rather than letting

change shape us are great challenges for school executives. As
the administrator looks at his institution in context with the rest
of society he must realize that we live in an era of explosive
change with resultant traumatic impact upon educational institutions. The planning and projecting activities in a university or
school system must utilize some of the new forecasting tools that
will keep the chief executive officer in contact with new forces
that will be changing education and educational practice.

Today's students, having grown up in an era of affluence, are
oriented to broader concerns than production or the necessities
of life and building economic security. They are concerned about
the quality of life, and they would hope to see our economy and
great economic power turn toward considerations that list material things in a lower place in the hierarchy of values.

Many scholars are joining these young people in demanding
that government try to help citizens to make their lives more
rewarding and self-fulfilling. Instead of merely seeking economic
plenty from wealth and production, government should concern
itself more about qualitative matters and the general human
condition. Education as the champion of the individual and the
advocate of building an individual's mind and spirit should be
taking the lead over all other governmental functions in this
move toward more self-fulfillment and deeper quality in the way
we live. We are, indeed, under-utilizing our abilities in many
aspects of life aside from that of producing material wealth and
economic plenty. The future-oriented school executive must be
cognizant of these needs as he directs the activities of his planners
in the development of future thrusts of MBO.

To be able to discern trends and to develop a keen and in-
sightful sense of timing are crucial attributes to be cultivated by
the school executive. He must, in short, be a strong advocate of
the old cliche that there is nothing more powerful than an idea
whose time has come. His leadership should be sufficiently future-
oriented to recognize those powerful new ideas that are timely
and that are suggesting that they need his attention.

The role of the chief executive officer in MBO calls for a constant reading of the feedback. Moreover, his behavior must be

such that he will encourage and keep the feedback coming to him. He needs to read the signals and feel the pulse of developments so that he can make necessary changes when feedback calls for it. Educational leadership has traditionally been very conservative and unusually hard to change. The future-oriented school executive should be keeping in close contact with unborn tomorrow. The future of his institution will, in large measure, depend upon his insightfulness in reading the real signs of social-futurism.

SUMMARY

This chapter has attempted to describe to the reader the complex and sensitive role of the chief executive officer in making MBO a truly effective force in reforming, renewing, and moving the school system or university in a direction commensurate with the timely needs and demands of society. The impact of the personal touch of the school executive and the importance of his mind and spirit functioning in a true leadership role have been emphasized. A large list of do's and don'ts has been presented. The do's include some very necessary and almost imperative roles and responsibilities that must be assumed by the chief executive. Most of them can be assumed by no one else. Considerable space has been devoted to the charisma and style of the chief executive in utilizing the MBO system to build unity, allegiance, and enthusiasm among the staff. Knowing that MBO can become a mechanical monster in management, considerable emphasis has been given to the leadership responsibility of the chief executive to see that MBO helps to seek out and meet the need for fulfillment of the lives of human beings. This has been done under the concept that education should be the most humane of all endeavors. The chief executive officer has a transcending obligation to see that his management system has a firm allegiance to humaneness.

10

Summary and Conclusion

ELEVEN STEPS IN THE MBO CYCLE

Modern-day school administration does not call for total performance of leadership genius but it does call for the ability to coordinate the efforts of many with varied talents and interests into a viable team. The team must be renewal oriented and capable of solving problems.

MBO is a management system that is particularly useful in coordinating the labors of a staff toward attainment of some common goals. The system, moreover, can easily be made to function in time phase around the typical calendar of an academic year that is common to universities and school systems.

The school executive must offer leadership in moving his organization through an MBO cycle as it solves problems and renews itself. This renewal through coordination of staff efforts over the extent of a yearly MBO cycle will be described in this chapter.

THE STEPS IN AN MBO YEAR

There are eleven steps in completing an MBO cycle during an academic year (see Table 1):

TABLE 1

MBO Planning Calendar

Steps in MBO Cycle	Typical Completion Deadline Date
Step 1 — Needs Assessment	By January 1, prior to beginning of next academic year.
Step 2 — Tentative Performance Priorities	By February 1, prior to beginning of next academic year.
Step 3 — Staff Critique of Tentative Performance Priorities	By March 1, prior to beginning of next academic year.
Step 4 — Final Performance Priorities	By March 15, prior to beginning of next academic year.
Step 5 — Departmental or School Unit Priorities	By April 1.
Step 6 — Written Objectives from Each Department or School Unit	By April 15.
Step 7 — Central Office Approval of Objectives	By May 1.
Step 8&9 — Final Objectives Written by Each Unit and Operational Planning Completed	By June 15.
Step 10 — Operational Execution of Time-Phased Action Steps	From opening of academic year until its close.
Step 11 — Year-End Review of MBO Accomplishments	As soon as possible after step 10.

1. Needs Assessment.

As described in an earlier chapter, the first step is to assess the needs of the institution or school system so that problems can be identified and some ideas formulated as to urgency and priority. The needs assessment should be completed approximately six months prior to the beginning of a new academic year. There must be adequate time for staff involvement and for subsequent staff participation and reaction as described in step two below.

In the first year of MBO the needs assessment effort may of necessity be limited to use of existing information and may have to be focused upon known problems. Since the first year will be a learning and adaptation effort, time and energy in needs assessment should be expended sparingly. After a year's experience the staff will be ready for a genuine needs assessment effort that will probe in depth into the problems of the organization. Keeping needs assessment simple so that MBO can be launched with the greatest simplicity will be essential to success the first year.

2. Tentative Performance Priorities.

When the chief executive issues his tentative performance priorities that have been formulated from the needs assessment the entire institution is given an opportunity to react, to help revise and formulate the final priorities. These tentative priorities — usually from five to seven in number — should be issued early enough to permit genuine staff response and earnest administrative attention to that response.

3. Staff Dialogue and Critique.

The tentative performance priorities will commit the staff to problem solutions that will affect the work of many during the coming academic year. The voice of the professional staff in determining the priorities that will occupy time and resources must be heard. The list of tentative performance priorities must be open to change, deletions, additions, and extensive revision. If the chief executive is not willing to give and take, the staff will not offer the quality of criticism essential to setting critical priorities for work during the coming year.

By at least four months prior to the beginning of a new academic year the staff response to the tentative performance priorities should be back to the chief executive's office.

4. Final Performance Priorities.

After studying the response, criticism, and suggestions for change, the chief executive should issue his final performance priorities for the coming academic year. As explained in Chapter 3 these priorities can and should be supplemented with departmental or school unit priorities. The final performance priorities should be issued as soon as possible following step three above. They must come out early enough to permit the staff work to be completed in setting school unit and departmental objectives and to permit adequate time for operational planning of time-phased action steps described in Chapter 5.

5. Departmental or School Unit Performance Priorities.

The department head or school principal should initiate an immediate examination and discussion of the system-wide or university-wide performance priorities upon receipt of the same from the chief executive's office. The unit staff members should be responsive to the system-wide priorities but they should also devise some of their own priorities aimed at problems of particular concern that may not be system wide in scope.

From an extensive discussion, a staff consensus should be reached as soon as possible after receiving the final priorities for the entire institution. From two to three months will be needed to write objectives and complete operational planning. This time requirement calls for a short time frame in the MBO calendar for setting school unit and departmental priorities.

6. Writing Objectives.

Following the detail outlined in Chapter 4 the school unit or department should write objectives that make performance commitments that are responsive to the system-wide priorities established in step five above. Great care should be taken in writing these objectives so that the staff will understand what commitments have been made, how they will be met, and by what dates the work will be accomplished. In the first year of MBO the major objectives should be limited to three to five. Since this will be a learning experience, they must be limited in scope and complexity. Most organizations with extensive experience in MBO recommend ten to twelve major objectives as the outside number that can be effectively managed.

7. Review and Approval of Objectives.

The local unit objectives should be submitted to the chief executive and his central office staff for review and approval. This central review will facilitate coordination of the efforts of the various units in the organization. It will eliminate duplication and overlap. With tight budgets, it will permit central allocation of resources on a priority basis.

Another important function of central staff review of local school unit or college departmental objectives is to check responsiveness to the chief executive's performance priorities. If the objectives submitted by the local unit fail to recognize a need to mount a special effort to correct a deficiency of particular concern to the institution and its mission, the unit head should be requested to justify his omission.

The central purpose of MBO is to solve problems and insure effectiveness in areas where the educational institution is weak. In the needs assessment effort these weaknesses will have been identified. Those units in the organization causing the deficiencies will also have been identified.

If, for example, a public school system's needs assessment reveals a weakness in student achievement in mathematics the central staff should be anticipating some major objectives from those school units with deficiencies in this area. If a unit ignores this priority despite the fact that its performance in the past has contributed to the district-wide deficiency, the superintendent's central staff should call the local administrator's attention to the district-wide problem and suggest that a major objective should be adopted to close the gap.

In lecturing to groups of school superintendents in leadership seminars in California the author was asked if he believed that objectives should be imposed upon a local school unit by the superintendent. When he responded that the objectives should be developed by the principal and his professional staff the question was then posed as to what the superintendent should do in circumstances where low achieving schools ignored performance priorities suggested by the superintendent. In such instances, the superintendent and his central staff should try to persuade the local unit personnel to recognize the problems that stand out for remedial action. An imposed objective will not have commitment from the staff. The leadership initiative should rest with the school principal with the central staff lending assistance in persuading the staff to assume responsibility for meeting a high priority need.

8. Unit Head and Staff Write Final Objectives for the Year.

After the central staff and the chief executive have approved the tentative objectives submitted by the local school units or college departments, the writing of major objectives as described in Chapter 4 should be completed. These objectives, when submitted to the chief executive in final form, become a performance commitment for the academic year. The objectives state explicitly what is to be accomplished by the end of the academic year. Hopefully, there has been extensive involvement by all the staff up to this decision point and the performance commitment has the full support of all staff members in the school unit or college department.

9. Operational Planning Is Completed.

Each local unit develops a detailed, time-phased operational plan to reach the major objectives for which performance commitments were made in step eight above. This operational planning includes the major milestone events and the time-phased action steps described in Chapter 5 of this book.

10. Operational Execution of the Action Steps Is Completed.

Through the ongoing efforts of the staff throughout the course of the academic year the operational plans in step nine are executed. This step in the MBO cycle is the big one that consumes most of the academic year. The management review conferences and other operational management activities described in Chapter 6 are carried out in step ten of the MBO cycle.

11. Year-End Review of MBO Accomplishments.

At the conclusion of the academic year the MBO accomplishments are reviewed. A detailed analysis of the objectives and of the executed action steps is completed. A final report on MBO is completed by each unit in the organization. This report should summarize accomplishments, identify those objectives fully met and those that were not met according to the operational plan.

The institution attempts at this point to teach itself from the experience of the past academic year. By being critically introspective about its operations the local units and the total system will gain management wisdom and skill to be used in a new MBO cycle the following year.

It is particularly important that the summary reports on MBO be widely circulated throughout the staff of each unit in the organization. If this step is missed staff members will not learn from the year's experience with MBO. Extensive discussion of the year's efforts should be encouraged as a prelude to launching a new MBO year.

LAUNCHING A NEW MBO YEAR

A self-renewing university or school system is constantly planning, implementing, evaluating and revising to reach increasingly higher levels of performance in renewing its student body and carrying out all aspects of its mission. MBO facilitates this procedure of institutional self-renewal. It provides the framework within which all managers and professional colleagues may operate.

The yearly needs assessment effort should be executed early enough before the opening of a new academic year to permit adequate time for planning and implementation of plans. With the staff involvement and participation decision-making requirements of MBO, the needs assessment effort must be executed well in advance.

The new performance priorities must evolve from the bottom up and from the top down. Keen interest and intensive debate should follow the needs assessment program as new priorities are set to guide the special problem-solving efforts that will occupy the attention of the institution for the new academic year.

As the school system or university launches each new MBO cycle the extent of involvement and the intensity of interest on the part of the staff will increase. The accumulation of several years of experience in system-wide planning, implementing, evaluating and revising under the management system should result in a very high level of skill and sophistication in utilizing the systems approach to management. The evaluation instruments should improve yearly and should ultimately lead to effective use of planning networks. Time and resource commitment procedures should also evolve (from the overly simplistic approaches described in this text on MBO fundamentals) to a much higher level of results-oriented decision making.

SUMMARY

This chapter has surveyed the steps in completing an MBO cycle. The fundamentals of results-oriented management through use of a management system should be more apparent to the reader after having reviewed these eleven steps in the annual MBO cycle. The self-renewing MBO process of planning, implementing, evaluating, and revising was described in the eleven-step cycle.

This is the process by which an institution assures that experience is instructive. This is the process that keeps the institution results oriented, young and dynamic in seeking ever increasing levels of effectiveness in reaching worthy goals of performance excellence.

Appendix A

Report of Assessment of Critical Educational Needs in Utah's Public Schools (and Assessment by the Division of Research and Innovation, Utah State Board of Education, Office of the State Superintendent of Public Instruction, Salt Lake City, Utah

IDENTIFYING UTAH'S CRITICAL
EDUCATIONAL NEEDS

A need, by casual definition, is a discrepancy between *what is* and *what ought to be*. More precisely, it is seen as an urgent requirement of something essential or desirable that is lacking.

In Utah, as in American society as a whole, there is substantial agreement on the general purposes of public education as evidenced by the reports of many committees and commissions who have studied the functions of the schools in the past several decades. Most recently Utah has been participating in an eight-state study, the purpose of which was to construct an educational design for the 1980's. One of the study committees of this project explicated objectives that would be appropriate for education of the future. These have been used as the definition of "what ought to be" for Utah's initial educational needs assessment activities. The central theme of these future goals for Utah public education, like other statements of this kind, is the maximum individual fulfillment of each Utahn.

Individual fulfillment can be thought of as having two major components: (1) fulfillment in work or a career, and (2) fulfillment in leisure time, cultural and recreational pursuits. It is believed that Utah's educational system of the future should be able to take for granted the satisfaction of such primitive drives as

147

Maslow's (1954) physiological and safety or security requirements. This would make it possible to concentrate on the higher
order drives in his hierarchy including affiliation or close effective relations and achievement and esteem. The desired condition
would be to enable each person to focus primarily on his highest
drive, self-actualization, involving full development of his potential in terms of skills, abilities, and appreciation (Flannigan
1968).

The second phase of Utah's needs assessment was to determine how well we are doing in relation to our educational objectives. It was decided to begin with a process that would harvest
the concerns of Utahns regarding their schools and to validate
the most critical concerns in terms of facts, values and policies.
This process has yielded four clusters of concerns:

1. Concerns about more adequately serving the unique needs
   of students, such as children of low income families, children of migrant farm workers, Indian children, children of
   non-English speaking parents, rural children, handicapped
   children, and school dropouts.
2. Concerns about educational objectives that are not being
   reached satisfactorily, such as reading abilities, knowledge
   management skills, human values, preparation for success
   in the world of work, and independence in learning self-
   concept.
3. Concerns about the processes of education.
4. Concerns about the cost effectiveness of certain educational practices and programs, such as class size, staffing
   patterns, special education, and special student services.

Each of these concerns has been analyzed and validated in
terms of relevant values, facts and policies. This process has identified Utah's critical educational needs which in turn have been
processed into statements of problems from which the priority
targets for Title III projects will be selected.

CONCERNS ABOUT LOW-ACHIEVING CHILDREN

A major concern of educators and public alike in Utah would
seem to be that some children are not being served by their

schools. It is the purpose of this section of the needs assessment report to assess the validity of this concern as it is expressed for Indian children, children from rural areas, children from low income families, handicapped children and school dropouts.

Values and Policies

Utahns place high value on education for every child. This value is expressed in Utah's efforts in education. Ninety-eight percent of its students attend school. It ranks #1 in the nation in terms of the attained educational level of its population.

Not only do Utahns value education, they also value equality of educational opportunity for every child. This value is expressed in finance laws for education where for years provision has been made for equalization factors designed to provide equality of educational opportunity for all children.

Utahns also value educational achievement. This is expressed in public statements by leaders in the state and also by the leading position in the educational achievement of its citizens.

Policy in Utah reflects the high value Utahns place on education. The law provides for compulsory education through high school or age 18. State financial support is predicated on the daily attendance of pupils. School district policies provide for the monitoring of attendance of each child.

In general it is fair to say that an effective education for every child is a value accepted in Utah and that there is no major discrepancy between this value and school policies in respect to it.

Facts

Facts relevant to the above values and policies as they relate to Indian children, to children from rural or low income families, handicapped children and school dropouts, do not match entirely those values and policies.

A. Indian Children

1. One study reports a 71.2% dropout rate for Indians in Southern Utah. The same study reports a total graduation

rate of 83.6 for all students in the same area. (*The American Indian Dropout in the Southwest*, Southwest Cooperative Education Laboratory, Albuquerque, New Mexico, 1968, page 14.)

2. A study quoted by Dr. Ed Moe, Bureau of Community Development, University of Utah, reports a dropout rate for Indian children in Utah of 70% compared with 15% for Orientals, 20% for whites, and 35% for Negroes.

3. A study by Philip Ellis four years ago in Uintah School District reported a dropout rate of 50% among Indian children from grade 9 to 12.

4. Nationwide, the dropout rate for Indian children has been estimated at 60% compared to the national average of 29%. (Dr. Alphonse D. Selinger, *The Northwest Indian After High School*, a paper presented at the NFIRE Conference in Denver, March 17, 1969.)

5. One study in 1965 of the relationship of measured ability levels to achievement levels of Indian and non-Indian students in Uintah County reported "with regard to the *SRA Achievement Series*, Indian males were found to score lowest in every test area. They were followed by Indian females, non-Indian males, and non-Indian females." (*A Comparative Study of the Relationship of Measured Ability Levels of Indian and Non-Indian Students in Uintah County, Utah*, Wells A. McInelly, University of Wyoming, Laramie, Wyoming, 1965, page 52.)

6. The study cited in #5 above concludes that:

   As a group, the Indian students in this study have not attained the same levels of measured ability and achievement as non-Indian students.

7. A follow-up study of the 1964-65 ninth grade students at West Junior High School in Vernal, Utah, reports 55.8% of the Indian students in that class failed to graduate as compared with 14.5% of the white students. (*Follow-up Study of 9th Grade Students, West Junior High* 1964-65, Uintah School District, Vernal, Utah 1969.)

8. The above study shows that 18 or 41.8% of the Indian students who were ninth graders in 1964-65 are presently

unemployed as compared with six or 10.9% of the white students.

9. The above study shows that ten or 23% of the Indian students were presently enrolled in some form of education beyond high school as compared with 20 or 36% of the white students.

10. Indian student attendance in Uintah School District is significantly below that of white student attendance. (*Attendance Reports*, Uintah School District, 1967-68.)

11. In Utah, teachers and others in schools with Indian enrollments consistently speak of the low levels of school achievement among Indian students. Such statements are available for listing.

12. At Union High School nine Indian graduates of a total of 17 Indian graduates of the class of 1968 entered college. At Christmas only two were still in college.

13. Nationwide, several sources make references to the low academic achievement of Indian students as compared with national norms. (Hildegard Thompson, *Today's Dropouts — Tomorrow's Problems*, Bureau of Indian Affairs, 1959. James D. Cowhig, "Characteristics of School Dropouts and High School Graduates, Farm and Non-Farm," U.S. Dept. of Agriculture, Economic Research Service, Agriculture Report #65, 1960, Washington, D.C.)

14. A study by the Northwest Regional Education Laboratory reports that only half of the graduates who entered post-high school programs completed them. The same study also shows that six years after graduation one-half were unemployed for pay or profit and two-fifths of those employed wished to change their jobs. (Northwest Regional Laboratory, *The American Indian Graduate: After High School What?* Portland, Oregon, 1968.)

B. Rural Children

1. "Students from Utah's larger high schools performed at a higher level on the ACT battery than their counterparts from small high schools." (*How Good Are Utah Public*

Schools? Utah State Board of Education, Salt Lake City, 1967, page 77.)

2. Small, rural schools produce fewer high achievers than do urban schools. In a study now being completed by Mark Simmons, University of Utah, of 396 small, rural high school students and 416 urban high school students, only 1 1/2% of the students from the small schools could be classified as high achievers while 7 1/2% of the urban students were so classified. I.Q. scores for each group did not differ significantly.

3. In 1967-68, course offerings in small, rural schools in Utah, 9-12, averaged 26 discrete offerings as compared with over 110 such offerings at Olympus High School. (Northwest Accrediting Association Reports on file at the State School Office.)

4. Offerings in certain subjects including foreign language, music, art, advanced mathematics, advanced science other than physics and chemistry, forensics, drama, vocational education and journalism are absent in about half of the small schools and are extremely limited in the others. (WSSSP *Study of Class Offerings in Small Schools*, 1966-68.)

5. In Utah it is estimated there are almost 38,000 children needing services in the area of special education. Of this about 20,000 are receiving some special education services and about 18,000 receiving no special education services. Most special education services are non-existent or extremely limited in rural areas, as evidenced by the following statistics from State Board of Education, *Special Education Report*, 1967:

a. Of the 17 school districts reporting no services provided for the educable, all 17 are rural districts.

b. Only three districts, all urban, provided services to the motor handicapped.

c. Nineteen school districts reported no services in the area of speech and hearing. All were rural.

d. No rural district provided services to the deaf.

e. Of the 26 districts reporting no services for the hard of hearing, 25 were rural districts.

f. Of the eight districts providing services to the emotionally maladjusted, only one could be classified as a rural district.

g. Of the 27 districts reporting no services to the trainable, 26 were rural.

6. Research seems to support the view that teachers rarely fail because of lack of knowledge. Rather they fail more often because of failure to transmit knowledge in a way that is meaningful to their students. Even so, where traditional patterns of teachers' behavior prevail, as in rural areas, there is widespread agreement that the teacher should be knowledgeable. It is difficult to find data that are valid in the assessment of teacher effectiveness in rural areas. However, those data we have indicate a lack in effective staffing in rural schools. Following are some of the relevant facts:

a. With the exception of homemaking and vocational agriculture, the number of teachers teaching subjects in which they have neither a collegiate major nor minor is significantly greater in small rural schools than in larger, urban schools. A majority of the math teachers in small schools have neither a major nor a minor in math. Only half of the language arts teachers have major or minor preparation in this subject. (Study by WSSSP for Utah, 1966-68.)

b. Proportionately there are significantly fewer teachers with advanced degrees in small schools than in large schools. (Study by WSSSP for Utah, 1966-68.)

c. Teacher turnover is significantly greater in small rural schools than in large urban schools. (Study by WSSSP for Utah, 1966-68.)

d. Teachers in small schools have fewer years of teaching experience than those in large schools. The percentage of first and second year teachers in rural schools is higher than in urban schools, but the percentage of teachers with over 20 years' experience is higher in rural schools. (Study by WSSSP for Utah, 1966-68.)

C. *Children from Low Income Families*

1. In Utah there are 17,467 students from low income families, according to a report of Title I Activities for the fiscal year ending June 30, 1968. It is possible that general nationwide reports on children from low income families will apply to those in Utah — at least, that is the assumption of the Title I program. The Coleman Report documents nationally the fact that low income minority groups are not being served by the schools. Mario Fantini, in the *Harvard Educational Review*, 1968, page 161, says: "The most visible failure (of public education) is in the low income minority groups."

2. Salt Lake City School District qualifies for Title I ESEA funds because of 4151 students enrolled from low income families. Total enrollment in Salt Lake City School District is 35,630. Granite School District qualifies for Title I ESEA funds because of 2157 students enrolled from low income families. Granite has a total enrollment of 61,787. Yet Salt Lake City School District reported 604 dropouts in 1967-68 compared with 397 reported in Granite School District. One explanation for this much higher dropout rate in Salt Lake is the larger number of children from low income families.

    The same explanation is made for the 313 dropouts last year in Ogden School District as compared with 162 in Jordan School District. Ogden enrolls 17,167 students, 1,394 of whom are classified as coming from low income families. Jordan serves 22,266 students, 784 of whom come from low income families. This provides some evidence of greater dropout rates among children from low income families.

3. A study published by the Salt Lake City School District in 1968 called *The Urban Picture* gives comparative achievement and dropout data on Inner City and the total city. Inner City is the area of most extensive poverty in Salt Lake City, the area from South Temple to 13th South and from 5th West to 7th East. Some of these comparisons are:

a. Inner City has a dropout rate 2 1/2 times larger than the city average.
b. Third grade achievement in Inner City is 3.3 compared with 4.0 for the total city.
c. Sixth grade achievement is 5.6 compared with 6.6 for the total city.
d. Average daily attendance is 92.7% in Inner City, 95% for the total city and 96% for Salt Lake County.
e. 23% of the total non-attenders in Salt Lake are in the Inner City which compares less than 10% of Salt Lake's student population.

D. Handicapped Children

The education of children with handicaps presents a special area of concern.

Data

1. Table 2 shows the extent to which handicapped children in Utah are presently being served.

Classification	Approximate No. of Students in the State in this Category	Approximate No. of Students in the State Being Served	Approximate % of Students in the State Not Being Served	No. of Districts Having No Prog. in this Category (of 40 Districts)
Educable	6,000	2,387	57%	14
Trainable	1,200	144	88%	32
Motor Handicapped	300	89	70%	35
Speech and Hearing	15,000	7,809	48%	17
Visually Handicapped	300	93	69%	36
Hard of Hearing	1,500	172	88%	39 (deaf) 33 (partially)
Emotionally Maladjusted	6,000	420	93%	31

TABLE 2

2. A selected group representing many areas of handicapping
    conditions reported to the State Advisory Council their
    perceptions of needed innovative programs to be consid-
    ered under Title III. These suggestions were listed on a
    questionnaire and sent throughout the state to personnel
    who work with handicapped children. They were asked to
    rank the suggestions. Those responding to the question-
    naire were:

a.	Teachers and/or Therapists	25
b.	Local District Special Edu-cation Administrators	10
c.	Parents and PTA Exceptional Child Chairman	8
d.	Superintendents and Principals	5
e.	State Administrators	4
f.	University Personnel	4
g.	Professional Teacher Organization	5

Table 3 is a tabulation of these responses:

Suggested Innovation	*Total Points: 3 for 1st, 2 for 2nd, 1 for 3rd*	*No. of times each innovation was ranked first*
a. Exemplary Procedures for Identification and Placement of the Handicapped	43	17
b. Exemplary Programs for the Emotionally Disturbed	39	15
c. Innovative Programs for Parents	33	10
d. Innovative Teaching Methods	28	
e. Model Programs for the Moderately Retarded	20	
f. Recreation for the Handicapped	19	

TABLE 3

Policy

Money is appropriated by the State Legislature to provide
special education services in special classes to *all* students of
the state who qualify for these services.

Value

The State policy for the aid of the handicapped indicates that great value is placed on the training of the handicapped. Lack of trained personnel makes service to all handicapped children impossible under present regulations related to the handicapped.

E. School Dropouts

There is a disproportionate percentage of students dropping out of school in urban school districts of Utah (Ogden and Salt Lake City).

Data

During the three school years of 1965-66, 1966-67, 1967-68, the combined dropout rate of 38 of Utah's 40 school districts declined; i.e., 1965-66 — 1.29%; 1966-67 — 1.24%; 1967-68 — .99%. During this same three-year period the combined dropout rate in the two urban districts of Salt Lake and Ogden increased 2.57%, 2.72% and 2.89%. In the Salt Lake City District there were 623 dropouts during the 1967-68 school year. A high percentage of these dropouts live in the area designated as "central city." In this area 58% of the students do not live with both parents; 23% of the city's non-attenders live in this area which makes up less than 10% of the population; more than 50% of the student bodies of some of these central city schools comes from the so-called minority groups.

Delinquency is high in central city: juvenile arrests among the 8-18 age group are 31.9% compared to 6.4% for the rest of the city; less than 6% of the city's 8-18 age group live in central city, yet 24% of total arrests in the age group are made from this group.

F. Needs Related to Low-Achieving Students

The mismatch between values and policies relevant to education in Utah and the relevant facts define the following problems with respect to the education of low achieving children:

1. Educational programs must be developed which will bring

relevant curriculum methods and materials to bear on the education of Indian children in Utah. Such programs must provide for achievement of these children in terms of their goals and those of the society in which they live.

2. Educational programs must be developed in rural areas which provide children in rural schools with educational opportunities to develop their potentials to the maximum. These should include making available to the rural child all the competencies, materials and learning opportunities needed for his success.

3. Educational programs must be developed that will deal with the special characteristics of children from low income families including low self-image, low educational aspirations and limited experimental background.

4. Programs that would meet the needs of handicapped children who reside in rural Utah and programs that extend the specialization know-how to those handicapped students not now being served should become targets for Title III projects.

5. Programs in the areas of early identification of potential dropouts, more viable programs for those identified based on diagnosis and prescription and a greater degree of "accountability" by school districts for successful completion of relevant programs should receive priority consideration.

Early Childhood Education

The education of children in the preprimary years has recently been the object of much research. Records show that nursery school education in the United States dates back to 1920 when three nursery schools were in existence; 25 had been established by 1924, one of them in a public school. By October 1966, enrollment of three-, four- and five-year old children in both public and private nursery schools had reached 686,000.

A number of problems and developments are of significance to early childhood education today. Interest in problems of school failure, dropouts, and socio-economic conditions is making strong impacts on education, particularly for the young child.

Early childhood education seems to be the growing edge of early elementary education today. The type of early childhood education which seems to have the greatest relevance to Title III, because of a critical educational need for which it seems to offer solutions, is that early education for the educationally disadvantaged child.

These schools are intended to reduce or eliminate educational retardation. Professional personnel in mental and physical health, welfare, recreation and parent education are usually involved in these projects, which are designed to provide the wide experiental background needed by children for success in our schools today.

This service is often provided for such groups as children of migrant workers, handicapped children and children whose family resources are so limited that books, games, educational materials and equipment are not a part of the young child's experience during his very early years.

The Head Start Program has done much to foster Early Childhood Education.

CONCERNS ABOUT EDUCATIONAL
OBJECTIVES NOT BEING MET
IN UTAH'S PUBLIC SCHOOLS

Although a good deal of the effort being expended on the production of Utah's educational product yields a good return, evidence of our falling short in several areas is all around. As we examine the concerns of educational groups and lay groups and the data supporting these concerns, the most pressing are in the following categories:

1. Humanizing education
2. Independence in learning
3. Success in the world of work
4. Reading skills
5. Intellectual skills (made up of inquiry and problem solving).

While we understand that instruction in many content areas contributes toward developing competencies of children in these areas, the efforts to date, as measured by the behavior students are now exhibiting, indicate we have taken more of a "flock shot" than a deliberate, sequential presentation of activities leading toward the accomplishment of these competencies. The notion that skill in inquiry and problem solving will result from posing content problems or inquiring into content domain doesn't necessarily follow. Likewise, skill in human relations and the ability to work independently do not necessarily result from working together in a classroom situation and being given some time for independent study.

On the other hand, we say society values these skills, yet there is not a deliberate structuring of the curriculum to obtain them, nor are there appropriate rewards when evidence of these things is exhibited. We rather award commendation and reinforcement for high performance in the content areas and in some competitive peripheral activity. Few of our efforts have been directed at resolving a mismatch of what we say we value and what we are deliberately producing with the present educational activities. Deeper than this is the problem that few of our activities have been directed towards deliberately producing a product or behavior that was well described.

If concerns about the children in Utah being able to excel in the areas of reading, inquiry, problem solving, human relations, independence in learning and the factors that bring success in the world of work are an accurate reflection of society's values, evidence of our present school program's ability to produce those competencies is lacking.

Facts

A. *Humanizing Education*

1. Many of our current problems of alienation and depersonalization are at least partly traceable to our emphasis in our schools upon giving and getting information and our neglect

of the discovery of meaning and humanization. The committee writing the 1962 ASCD Yearbook listed 13 common school practices that have depersonalizing and alienating effects:

- The emphasis on fact instead of feelings
- The belief that intelligence is fixed and immutable
- The continual emphasis upon grades, artificial reasons instead of real ones for learning
- Conformity and preoccupation with order and neatness
- Authority, support and evidence
- Solitary learning
- Cookbook approaches
- Adult concepts considered as the only ones of value
- Emphasis on competition
- Lockstep progression
- Force, threat and coercion
- Wooden rules and regulations
- The age-old idea that if it's hard it's good for them.

2. Until now we have been schooling to fit a "norm" of society. It's time to begin thinking of an education for every man. As defined by Carl R. Rogers, "The only man who is educated is the man who has learned how to learn; the man who has learned how to adopt and change; the man who has realized that no knowledge is secure, that only the process of seeking knowledge gives a basis for security."

This clearly invalidates our conception of a successful student as one who simply graduates with a degree and a high grade point average — a molded, shaped figure ready to slip away from life and learning into the split-levels and station wagons of suburbia.

The repercussions of this "training" are now being felt. Students are dropping out of school and life because of their inability to reconcile education and reality. Individuality and imagination are frowned upon by many teachers who care more for and reward the "correct" answer. They stifle a child's initiative and teach him to slide by on what seems to be the correct and only way to perform.

3. We value living together harmoniously, yet since 1963 more than 10,000 school age children annually appear before the juvenile courts.

   a. Stealing accounts for 2,153 cases before authorities.
   b. Carelessness or mistakes of a drastic nature account for 1,802 cases.
   c. Running away from home accounts for 1,158 of the cases (half of them girls).
   d. Smoking and drinking account for 180 of the cases before the juvenile courts.
   e. Aggravated truancy contributed 612 offenses.
   f. More serious offenses of burglary and unlawful entry were involved in 609 cases.
   g. 519 were judgments made for stealing automobiles.
   h. Assault cases involving bodily injury accounted for 202 cases.

4. Juvenile population, age 12 to 17 in Utah, is approximately 250,000 and about one out of 20 of them appear before the juvenile courts each year. Incidence of juvenile population appearing before the court has increased 62% in the last ten years.

B. *Independence in Learning*

1. From an 18-school sample of 53 teachers and their students, only 2.6% of time involves students operating independently, asking questions for facts, definitions and explanation or assistance.

2. The student information system data of 1967 reveal teacher opinion on the matter at 3.85 or slightly above average. However, on some key items taken individually, the results are quite low. For example, on the item "likes to do things by himself," the summary shows 4.58 and by female only 4.77; "generates new ideas," 4.19; "well organized," 4.19; "creative," 4.10; "ability to generalize," 4.17; and "catches on quickly," 4.02 — all of which are below average.

C. *Success in the World of Work*

1. Out of 17,814 high school senior students enrolled in the State of Utah, 11,259 students completed vocational programs in the 1967-68 school year.
2. 7,462 of those who completed vocational programs were contacted in September 1968 following graduation.
3. 1,290 were employed full or part time in the area of their vocational training.

   a. Of those, 619 were employed full time at the same or closely related occupation as they were trained for. Students were excluded.
   b. 671 were employed part time in the area they were trained for or closely related area.

4. 4,020 continued full time in post-secondary schools.

   a. 1,004 continued in post-secondary schools in the same or related vocational field.
   b. 533 of the 1,004 were in vocational or technical non-degree programs.

5. Of a sample of 380 non-vocational high school students contacted in September following graduation in 1968, 157 were employed (37 full time, 120 part time); 223 were not employed; and 276 were in college.
6. A total of 3,016 students who completed vocational programs in high school are enrolled in post-secondary school programs in the area of their high school training.

D. *Reading*

1. An average of 38.5% of school children in Utah score below the fiftieth percentile in total reading ability.
2. There is a general trend toward decreased performance as the grade increases.
3. In the largest district of the state 1.3% of the students are reading more than one grade below level at the third grade; 6.5% at the fifth grade; and 11.6% at the sixth grade.
4. In the 1967-68 school year, 3% of the total state school

population were in remedial programs — almost all of which are remedial reading. This is some 9,170 students.

5. 26.2% of first grade students are below grade level and 50.9% of twelfth grade students are below grade level.

6. At a recent curriculum conference in the state only two areas of concern received more votes than reading as the number one priority.

E. Intellectual Skills

1. Even though the literature is replete (Fare and Shaftel, 1967; Hunkins, 1966; Seagoe, 1967) in pointing out that learning is of better quality and quantity where the student is involved in an inquiry or problem-solving situation, we continue to find a high percentage of classroom activities devoted to asking for facts, asking procedural questions, giving directions, defining and attending to routine and supervision.

2. In an 18-school sample involving 53 teachers and their classes, problem-solving procedures described or carried out by students were initiated by teachers only 1.1% of the time and initiated or volunteered by students only nine-tenths of one percent of the time. This included opportunities provided by the teacher to solve a problem presently or in the future. Insofar as inquiry is characterized by the descriptor "inquisitive, questions for facts, ability to generalize, resourcefulness, keeps at things, adjusts to new situations, generates new ideas, catches on quickly and is thorough," one must conclude that we do only an average job. The average of those nine descriptors on the Utah State Board Student Information System was 3.82.

3. The UASCD conference on priorities placed "a continuing interest in current problems, tendency to seek solutions and the habit of weighing alternatives and creatively applying them to the solution of these problems as the number one priority for educational effort in Utah today."

Values and Policies

The school has the responsibility to perpetuate the society through teaching those competencies, skills and attitudes that the society values. Utahns have expressed concerns related to competence in intellectual skills, human relations, independence in learning, success in the world of work and reading. If it is a well-endorsed policy that students in Utah have competence in these areas, programs must be designed to deliberately produce these skills. There is growing sentiment that the school be held accountable to show evidence that they are producing these characteristics in students. If present programs are not successful in doing this, as the data would suggest, there exists a mismatch between the produce we seek (value) and the product we are turning out. There also exists an ambiguity between concerns for achievement and concerns for emotional health. As programs are developed, they must produce the product we seek without damaging effects to emotional adjustment.

Needs Related to Educational Objectives

Educational programs need to be developed that will:
1. Humanize education by:
   a. Fully recognizing individual talents, abilities and interests and design learning activities that uniquely utilize these and promote their full development.
   b. Developing a humane environment in the school that values human worth, promotes respect and teaches human values.
2. Produce a high opportunity level for inquiry and problem-solving practices related to in-life problems.
3. Produce accountability in students for behavior individually and in groups.
4. Produce a management capability in each student for establishing and monitoring his own learning progress.
5. Create an awareness of occupational possibilities and identify the factors which have led to success by those who are well adjusted on their job.

6. Reorient preparation for employment so that:
   a. The objective of vocational education is the develop-
      ment of the unique individual employment interests.
   b. Preparation for employment is flexible and capable of
      adapting to individual needs in relation to the changing
      labor market.
   c. The system for occupational preparation will supply a
      salable skill at any terminal point chosen by the indi-
      vidual without closing doors to future progress and
      development.
   d. Some type of formal occupational preparation is a part
      of every educational experience.
   e. Intellectual competence and manipulative skills are not
      dichotomized.

CONCERNS RELATED TO THE
PROCESSES OF EDUCATION

One of the central concerns of educators, students and
school patrons is the limited extent to which school experiences
produce useful learnings and meanings for behavioral changes
in students. There is general awareness that the traditional teaching process, that has as its goal helping students accumulate
masses of verbal information, is simply not having extensive
influence in the out-of-school behavior of students.

Learning can be thought of in two ways: (1) as a separate
process or activity which can be carried on in a classroom independently of the out-of-school behavior it is intended to influence; and (2) as a change which occurs in behavior as a result of
the operation of that behavior under normal life conditions. The
first concept is illusory and leads to academic activities which
have little direct effect on life behavior. The second concept
agrees more closely with psychological analytical descriptions.

A second concern related to the educational process has to
do with the inability of the school to develop means and methods
that actualize the latent powers and potentialities of individual
students. Advanced knowledge and technology have convinced

both the scientific community and the public of the fact, with all its implications, that man functions at a small fraction of his capabilities.

Research conducted over the last 30 years has shown that there are many types of giftedness other than the commonly accepted "academic" giftedness. Creative talents, communication talents, planning talents and decision-making talents, for example, are known to exist. Furthermore, those who are high achievers in one of these talent areas may be only average or even low in another. Conversely those students whom we have been classifying as "slow learners" or "below average" may actually be above average if our standard were designed to measure, and our instructional programs focused to develop, talents other than the academic.

Closely allied to this concern is one relative to meeting the diversified needs of individual students. When the curriculum is lock-step, when there are few or no alternatives for students with varying abilities, when there is a single standard of performance for all students and students are required to progress at the same rate, many students fail and others are unchallenged.

A third major concern is lack of agreement between traditional teaching methods and learning psychology. While it is generally recognized that intuitive knowledge about teaching is operationally powerful, it is, however, inarticulate and inefficient. When teachers design instructional programs without an understanding of sound principles of learning, material selected for students to learn may be poorly structured and unsuited to the learner, learning procedure may be inefficient, retention might be low, transfer will be minimum and negative and motivation will be inadequate.

A fourth concern arises over the lack of skill many teachers exhibit in those classroom behaviors which are generally supported by research to be essential to effective instruction. Lack of skill on the part of the teacher generally results in an excess of teacher talk, overemphasis upon lower cognitive student responses and little decision-making or problem-solving experience for the learner.

Facts, Values and Policies

Because the education process is more related to the means for solving more basic educational problems, the validity and criticality of these concerns are found in the facts, values and policies relevant to the other three concern areas. However, there is ample research evidence to justify concern for the educative process. Some of the best known and respected studies that document this area of concern include:

Taylor, Calvin W.	— "Climate for Creativity," 1968
Otto, Herbert A.	— "Explorations in Human Potentialities," 1966
Woodruff, Asahel D.	— "A Teaching Behavior Code," 1969
Borg, Walter R.	— "The Mini-Course as a Vehicle for Changing Teacher Behavior, the Research Evidence," 1969

Needs Related to the Processes of Education

1. There is a need for curricula designed around a multi-talent approach to education that would reach those talents not being properly developed in the present academic program.
2. Training programs for teachers are critically needed that will (1) improve their competence in making instructional decisions that correctly apply psychological principles of learning and instruction, and (2) specifically train teachers for skill in essential classroom behaviors.
3. In order to optimize behavior change and transfer, a repertoire of learning tasks should be designed, each of which will allow the student to engage in carrying out a piece of in-life behavior, under realistic conditions, working with actual referents, making and executing his own decisions and being affected by the consequences of his actions. In this type of curriculum pattern, needed concepts and competencies are learned as a byproduct of the student's adjustmental efforts as he pursues these want-serving tasks.

4. Instructional systems for individualized instruction need to be developed. These must include: (1) learning materials suitable to a wide variety of abilities, interests and learning styles, (2) appropriate teaching behavior and instruction methods, and (3) classroom management procedures that allow for continuous progress and differentiated instruction.

COST EFFECTIVENESS —
A PRIORITY EDUCATIONAL CONCERN

Millions of dollars are spent each year in Utah for the conduct and improvement of public education, yet the quantity and quality of education available to many is believed inadequate to meet the educational aspirations of Utahns. Since the human and physical resources are limited, and those potentially usable for the improvement of the schools are competed for by other social needs, only limited resources are available for schools. When improvements are desired and only limited amounts of the necessary resources are available, the efficiency of resource allocation becomes a critical problem.

Efficiency is a rationality concept which suggests getting the most out of the least. Because learning is the goal of education, efficiency in education results when learning is maximized for any given investment of resources. The relative efficiency or rate of return on an investment for alternative educational programs, or effectiveness per cost expended, can be computed. Theoretically, both costs and effectiveness can be measured, but there are many practical difficulties. At least costs can be determined either as estimates in advance on the basis of budget allocations or as actual expenditures after the fact. The assessment of effectiveness or the prediction of effectiveness is much more difficult, however. Yet without some indication of predicted or resultant effectiveness there is no basis for deciding between one educational program and another.

A program's impact on grades (achievement), on the number and quality of graduates and dropouts, on future or predicted success in jobs, continued education and society are meaningful measures of effectiveness in terms of the student.

It would probably be desirable to measure the impact of educational programs on the community as well as on the student. Thus, both community economic and social effects should be elements in any measures of effectiveness. For example, economic benefits may be indicated in terms of changes in students' prospective income or lifetime earnings as a result of any identified educational program, and the social impact of a given program may be measured by determining if the predictability of educational achievement (behavioral change) for any classified group of students (low income, rural, handicapped) has declined as a result of the program.

Few educational improvement programs have been subjected to analysis as to their contribution to educational cost-effectiveness. New programs for increased effectiveness have usually been caught up in an "add-on" syndrome. Thus programs for benefiting handicapped children, dropouts, low-achieving students, etc., have been added on to the traditional school program.

Also, few attempts have been made to reduce costs of regular programs as a way of freeing resources for redeployment in the interests of increased effectiveness.

Facts

1. Education in rural, sparsely populated areas of the state costs more than it does in districts serving metropolitan areas of the state.

   — Daggett spends $1,177.06 per pupil while Murray operated its elementary secondary schools for $449.31 per pupil.
   — Seventeen "urban" districts spend less than $500 per pupil while five rural districts have per-pupil expenditures that exceed $700 a year.

2. Educating handicapped children in special education classes adds to the per-pupil costs of education.

— 2302 educable children require 209 teachers (FTE) at an estimated per pupil cost of $822 per student. These students are not included in regular programs.*

— 9023 children are enrolled in remedial reading classes. The estimated cost per pupil of this program is $312. But because these children are also enrolled in regular programs, this cost is an addition to the cost of the regular program. Thus the cost of educating children needing remedial instruction also exceeds $800 per pupil.*

— Approximately 100 speech and hearing teachers provide special help to 9,032 children, adding $100 per student to the cost of the regular program for each of these children.*

— 22,093 handicapped children participate in special education programs that employ 735 teachers (FTE). Approximately 3,700 of them are in special classes and thus are not enrolled in regular programs. Three hundred seven teachers are employed in these special classrooms. The remaining 18,000 (approximately) exceptional children are enrolled in regular classrooms and attend special education classes as a part of their total instructional programs.*

3. Seventy-six percent of the total instructional costs in Utah is for teachers' salaries.
4. Utah teacher salaries are considerably below the national average.
5. Most follow-up studies of pupils who receive remedial instruction indicate no significant improvement in long-term educational progress.
6. There is a growing body of literature questioning the effectiveness of special classes for handicapped children.
7. The resultant costs to society because of inadequately trained and poorly educated citizens in terms of low productivity, welfare care, cost of crime, etc., far exceed the additional costs of special education or other types of rehabilitative or compensatory education.

---

*These per-pupil costs were derived by dividing amount appropriated from the uniform school fund by number of pupils in the program.

Values and Policies

Equality of educational opportunity is a constitutional right of every school-age child in Utah. This policy requires larger expenditures for educating students who are slow achievers, are low in motivation, and suffer learning disabilities.

Also, Utahns place high value on programs that have great benefit in terms of the sociological as well as the vocational needs of society. Thus, even the rehabilitation of the severely handicapped must include more than vocational training.

Utah sends most of its children to the public schools (98%). In addition, Utah families average more school-age children per family than any other state. The percentage of its population in school is the highest in the nation. As a result Utah's per-pupil expenditure ranks 37th in the nation.

On the other hand there is growing taxpayer resistance to increases in taxation. The computer is being seriously considered as a viable tool for increasing educational effectiveness. The computer and computer programs are costly. The appropriate role of the computer in education has yet to be clearly defined.

Needs Related to Cost Effectiveness

A. Educational programs need to be developed that will:
1. Provide more economical ways of delivering quality educational services to rural students.
2. Increase the effectiveness of "regular" classrooms in effectively dealing with the unique needs of handicapped children and low achievers.
3. Raise teachers' salaries and teacher competence without greatly increasing total educational costs.
4. Optimize learning for each child without appreciably increasing instructional costs.
5. Make learning more productive and relevant in terms of critical economic and sociological needs of society, e.g., participation in democracy, human relationships, productive employment, lifetime learning, problem-solving skills.
B. Viable uses of modern technology, including the computer, should be explored as means to increase the effectiveness and/or reduce the costs of educational programs.

Appendix B

Sample Statements of Major Objectives for University, College, High School, Junior High School, and Elementary School Levels of Educational Management

UNIVERSITY RESEARCH PROPOSAL
OBJECTIVE — STATEMENT OF MAJOR OBJECTIVE

Problem Description:

The number of research grants received by the College of Physical Sciences from governmental and private sources has been steadily declining. Over the past five years the number of new grants received has declined from a high of 27 five years ago to only 13 last year. Moreover, the dollar amount of grants received has declined from $3.6 million to only $1.4 million. This decline appears to be related to the number of proposals prepared and submitted by faculty members to foundations, corporations, and governmental agencies. While 64 proposals were submitted five years ago, only 22 proposals were submitted last year. This trend must be reversed if the college is to continue to be effective in the area of research.

Statement of the Objective:

By the end of the coming academic year, the faculty of this college will have submitted not less than 55 high quality research proposals. (Details will be developed by a special committee on research to be appointed by the Dean.)

COLLEGE DROPOUT PREVENTION OBJECTIVE — STATEMENT OF MAJOR OBJECTIVE

Problem Description:

In the College of Engineering, 57% of the total students enrolled in the previous academic year either dropped out of engineering program by transfer to another college department or dropped out of the university. There is a need for more selectivity in admissions to the College of Engineering, better counseling and orientation during the initial weeks of each term, and more individualized instruction and personalized assistance. A 57% dropout and transfer rate is wasteful of both student and faculty time.

Statement of the Objective:

By the close of the next academic year, the percentage of students dropping out or transferring from the College of Engineering will be reduced from 57% to 45%. This percentage will be calculated the same as for the previous year. Our objective will be to reduce the dropouts and transfers from 57% of the total number of students enrolled in the next academic year to 45%. (In drawing up the time-phased action steps and in the operational planning for this objective, each of the four departments of the college will be given specific sub-objectives to help the college meet its major objective.)

HIGH SCHOOL ATTENDANCE OBJECTIVE — STATEMENT OF MAJOR OBJECTIVE

Problem Description:

For the past school year the average daily attendance at this high school was 89.5%. The attendance has been steadily declining each year. Absenteeism results in loss of student interest and commitment to learning. It causes problems for faculty in helping students to make up work and instruction missed because of absence. The school system receives state aid on the basis of average daily attendance. Loss of attendance causes the school district to lose money.

Statement of the Objective:

By the end of the coming academic year the average daily attendance at this high school will have been increased from 89.5% to not less than 91.5%.

HIGH SCHOOL CAREER EDUCATION OBJECTIVE — STATEMENT OF MAJOR OBJECTIVE

Problem Description:

Less than 50% of the graduates of this high school attended college or entered another institution of learning or training after high school graduation. The high school has an obligation to help all graduates to make meaningful post-high school choices. This is increasingly difficult for students who have no further contact with an educational institution after high school.

Statement of the Objective:

Beginning with next year's sophomore class, every tenth grade student will be given a comprehensive orientation to the world of work under a program to be developed by the counseling staff. Each tenth grade student next year will spend at least nine hours in the career orientation center and will complete a detailed and comprehensive investigation into at least eight occupational reference stations in the center.

JUNIOR HIGH SCHOOL DRESS STANDARDS OBJECTIVE — STATEMENT OF MAJOR OBJECTIVE

Problem Description:

Both parent and faculty groups have been complaining about the physical appearance of the students who attend this junior high school. Students have been coming to school in very "grubby" clothes. It seems to be popular among the students to wear clothing that is extremely worn, faded, patched over, and torn. It is believed that this trend has resulted in a dramatic increase in conduct problems. Parents who visit the school get an impression that is not truly representative of the quality of the students or the faculty.

There are no statistics to quantify this problem, but the expressed concern of parents and faculty makes it important that the problem be solved. If possible, the solution should come from the students' recognition of a need to do something to improve the "image" of the school. Dress standards that are rigidly imposed by the administration may result in resentment and defiance. Since it is an educational institution, educational procedures should be used.

Statement of the Objective:

The standard of dress and overall physical appearance of the students attending this junior high school will be substantially improved during the coming academic year. Since "substantially improved" is a somewhat nebulous term and since it is hard to measure an outcome such as this, a panel of parents and faculty members will be appointed to monitor the progress of the school in reaching this objective. (The student body officers will serve as consultants to the panel.) This objective will have been accomplished if the panel reports that there has been a substantial improvement in the dress and physical appearance of the student body of this school.

ELEMENTARY SCHOOL ACADEMIC ACHIEVEMENT OBJECTIVE — STATEMENT OF MAJOR OBJECTIVE

Problem Description:

Achievement in arithmetic in this school is 1.2 below the national norms as measured by the Stanford Achievement Test.

Achievement of students in grades one through three is slightly above the national norms. But achievement in grades four through six is below the national norms, and the lag in achievement becomes greater for grade five as compared to grade four and for grade six as compared to grade five.

Statement of the Objective:

By the end of the current academic year the achievement in arithmetic in grades four, five, and six in this school will have been increased by not less than six-tenths of a grade level as measured by the Stanford Achievement Test. (It is the intent of the faculty to bring achievement up to the national norms over a two-year period, and this objective will have closed the gap at least by one-half at the end of this academic year.)

ELEMENTARY SCHOOL INVOLVEMENT OF PARENTS
OBJECTIVE — STATEMENT OF MAJOR OBJECTIVE

Problem Description:

Less than 10% of the patrons of this school visit or contact the school each month. Additionally, less than 10% of the patrons are contacted by the faculty each month.

There is a need to involve the parents of children attending this school in the ongoing teaching and learning activities and to establish a closer working relationship with parents.

Statement of the Objective:

By the end of the coming academic year, every parent will have been contacted and invited to visit the school; each teacher will contact the parents of all children in the room at least twice and will have discussed the school's educational program; and a record of parents not contacting the school or responding to invitations will have been identified and the principal will make at least one personal telephone call to invite such parents to participate in the educational program.

ELEMENTARY SCHOOL SUMMER SCHOOL
OBJECTIVE — STATEMENT OF MAJOR OBJECTIVE

Problem Description:

The school district administration has allocated $50,000 to this school to conduct an experimental summer school program during the coming summer school season. The faculty and parents have not had any previous experience in planning and executing a summer school program. Despite the fact that the only statistic available is that $50,000 is available for a summer school program and that some district guidelines have been developed, this is a major problem facing the school that needs to be solved by application of the MBO procedure.

Statement of the Objective:

By the end of the coming summer season, and prior to the opening of the next academic year, 25% of the student body will have attended a summer school session of not less than six weeks in length under a program of instruction to be adopted by the Board of Education.

GUIDE FOR RECORDING A
MANAGEMENT OBJECTIVE

WEST HARTFORD PUBLIC SCHOOLS

GUIDE FOR RECORDING A MANAGEMENT OBJECTIVE

Principal ___Elizabeth H. Wrenn_____   School___King Philip Elementary

Date _____September 26, 1972_____

MANAGEMENT OBJECTIVE #1

By January 1, 1973, to build community and school understanding and support of the school renovation program--such program to be initiated no later than October 1.

STANDARDS OF PERFORMANCE (Measurable criteria including involvement of others)

1. No later than October 15, 1972 to convene a meeting of the King Philip Elementary School's building committee to bring the members up to date on the school upgrading program and to plan a strategy for developing understanding and support among King Philip families for the Bond Issue.

2. The October, November, and December Bulletins will carry information about the upgrading program looking toward developing understanding and support for the program.

3. At the October P.T.A. Board meeting, the principal and members of the Building Committee will discuss the specifics of the upgrading program and urge support.

4. No later than October 15, the upgrading program will be explained to the King Philip faculty by a member of the central office staff.

5. No later than November 15, the Building Committee will meet with the principal and other members of the parent group to develop a strategy for getting out the vote in the event of a referendum in January.

6. No later than December 15, the Building Committee will meet again to perfect its plan to get out the vote in anticipation of a possible referendum.

7. One week before the referendum, if any, the Building Committee working with the principal, faculty and selected members of the P.T.A. will meet to finalize the plan for getting the vote -- e.g. to implement the strategy developed in November.

MEASUREMENTS TO BE APPLIED

1. File the following reports with the Superintendent of Schools:

    a. minutes of all meetings as evidence of the quality of the planning and the extent of participation of each concerned group.

    b. copies of newsletters for October, November, and December.

2. The number of voters in the King Philip District who come out and vote for the Bond Issue, if and when a referendum is held.

RESULTS *

PERFORMANCE RATING *

---

*To be completed in April-May.

Appendix C

**Performance Priorities of the
Granite School District MBO System**

AN INTRODUCTION TO GRANITE SCHOOL DISTRICT
MANAGEMENT BY OBJECTIVES PROJECT

1. Benefits Derived from an MBO Program

Management by objectives is an approach to making the planning and execution of school operations more universally understood by all school staff members and to encourage the staff to focus more attention on outputs and results. An MBO system, if properly implemented with involvement of the staff, should create a sense of unity and teamwork in the school. Results-oriented management assures the staff that the school is aware of its problems and is concentrating on solutions. It generates interest because progress is well known, and this sense of momentum causes enthusiasm.

2. Plans for Initial Learning Experience

The Granite School District will initiate some first steps in gaining some of the positive benefits from MBO during the school year 1971-72. This will be a learning experience, and only a limited number of objectives will be adopted for deliberate management to accomplishment as we learn what MBO is all about. Hopefully, this will prepare us for the next year when a more fully implemented effort can be launched.

3. *Performance Priorities Suggested by the Superintendent*

Each year the Superintendent will suggest some performance priorities that reflect some district-wide needs. These may not, however, be the most urgent educational needs of a particular school. Each school should consider these performance priorities carefully but other priorities should also be considered. The Principal and his staff should set the objectives to be included as MBO system targets for the year. This should be done, however, after careful consideration of district-wide priorities.

As an initial experience it is recommended that three top priority objectives be adopted as school-wide educational outcomes. This does not mean that only these outcomes are important. It simply identifies the objectives to be systematically pursued as a learning experience in attaining expertise in MBO operations and as a means of setting and striving to attain some highly desirable school goals.

On the pages that follow are district performance priorities described briefly to communicate educational needs as viewed from the perspective of the Superintendent's office. These are not presented in any order of priority.

PERFORMANCE PRIORITY DESCRIPTIONS FOR GRANITE SCHOOL DISTRICT MBO SYSTEM

School Attendance

One of the first indicators of failure in school is poor attendance. Studies of dropouts and of students in trouble almost always show a high correlation with poor attendance. School attendance percentages have been declining in recent years on a nationwide scale. Some thoughtful observers consider this phenomenon to be part of the alienation of students from school and from society in general.

Poor school attendance leads to discouragement as the student faces makeup work and breaks in the continuity of the school program. Some parents do very little to encourage regular school attendance. This magnifies the necessity for the school to do all it can to reach chronic absentees and encourage regular attendance.

In the Granite School District approximately 5,000 students are absent from school each day. This represents an educational loss that is hard to comprehend. Additionally, it represents a huge dollar loss to the school system. This can be easily calculated in dollars for the district and for the individual school when it is realized that for every 27 students in average daily attendance the State guarantees approximately $11,600 and that 1/9 should be added to this for non-teaching services such as counseling, librarian and school administration units.

A cursory examination of Granite School District attendance shows that the per cent of attendance has been steadily declining over the past ten years. We should study the "magnetism" of each school to attract and hold its students in regular attendance. The loss in educational terms and in the future potential of each person is enormous and far outweighs the dollar loss referred to above.

There are schools in Utah with attendance percentages that reach 98% of enrollment. If the Granite system as a whole reached that level the average daily attendance would rise from 58,000 to 61,000. This may be an objective set too high to be realistic for an urban center. However, some schools should find it attainable and others should seek ways to increase attendance to the 97 or 96% range. A school with 800 enrollment with more than 16 students absent on a given day will quickly recognize that such attendance — if typical for the year — will place the institution below the very best attendance records of some schools.

Any school that adopts improved attendance as a major objective should be cognizant of negative side effects. If the program to generate better attendance causes students who are ill or who should be absent for good reason to attend school under pressure, negative results will ensue.

Every school in the Granite system should consider the improvement of school attendance as a matter of great concern. Those school units that set out in a planned, systematic program to improve attendance will be serving a number of needs of high priority and deep concern in the Granite School District.

Correction of Basic Study Skill Deficiencies

Schools should be oriented to faculty-wide analysis of student failure in basic study skill areas such as reading, mathematics, etc. There are certain minimum levels of proficiency that must be attained by every student if he is to have the basic keys to personal attainment. By looking at test data such as reading achievement scores, specific problems can be identified and attacked on an individual basis.

An objective in this priority area is difficult to quantify. It is, however, a very vital performance priority for schools — particularly for elementary schools. A certain level of intelligence and a certain degree of emotional and attitudinal adjustment seem to be vital to learning in the *regular* school program from typical methods and materials.

Schools adopting this objective indicate a "zero defects" concern that every child reach at least a minimum level of proficiency. Unusual problems require extraordinary methods and special attention to needs on an individualized basis.

Fortunately, there is a rich resource of materials and a great amount of research expertise in the basic study skill fields. A school faculty that commits itself to raise the level of the bottom 10 or 15% of its student population is accepting a challenge to eradicate future welfare recipients, wasted lives, and frustrated human outlook. A very tough minded "can do" attitude must accompany the school with courage to adopt eradication of basic study skill deficiencies as a performance priority in the MBO system. It is a difficult challenge, but a rewarding opportunity.

Schools having concentrations of low income and minority students should give strong consideration to this performance priority. It applies, however, to every school, for there are basic study skill deficiencies found in all student population groups.

Dropout Prevention

This performance priority relates to attendance and allied efforts to generate student interest and commitment to school.

Student dropout rates have been declining in the district, but there is still need for attention to this problem. This objective is, of course, more closely related to secondary education than it is to the elementary school program.

A dropout prevention objective should be developed with an awareness of the causes of student dropout. It should analyze ways of reaching the discouraged and disturbed student on a very personal basis. Students who appear to be potential dropouts should be identified and efforts made to change the school's strategy for meeting their needs and interests. Teachers may want to accept a challenge to work with certain individuals on a very personal basis to learn of problems at home and at school that need attention.

Unique and unorthodox approaches to planning and executing school experiences that will reach discouraged and disinterested students should be considered in appraising the performance of a secondary school relating to its ability to attract and hold students through effective programs designed to reach problem students. Most schools can succeed with highly motivated students from stable and supportive homes. The real challenge is to reach and hold the problem youth and nurture his development so that he can have a better, richer, and more rewarding life.

Outreach

Outreach is a term in education receiving increasing emphasis in recent years. It denotes the effort of a school to gain support, understanding, and involvement of the home and community in the educational program of the school.

Outreach recognizes that student achievement is enhanced when parents have close and continuous contact with the school. Outreach makes a special effort to reach the home of children having difficulty in adjusting to the school program.

The entire community school movement is part of an outreach objective. Parent-teacher conferences are part of this effort. Programs that draw parents to the school and contacts that increase ease of discussion and promote understanding become key elements in a school's outreach objective.

When parents become identified with a school and its program to the extent that a personal commitment is made, the school has gained an advocate and co-worker in support of education. Parents should feel entirely at ease and fully welcome at school. A first-name conversation relationship among school staff members and parents is helpful and should be encouraged. Outreach attempts to attain this type of informal rapport.

Needless to say, the PTA program does much to help schools in improvement of outreach performance.

In quantifying outcomes of an outreach objective, the number of individual contacts of teachers, counsellors and administrators should be considered as well as group programs and parent-teacher conferences. In planning the action steps the school staff should consider additional efforts that will increase the school's ability to reach more parents and improve the interpersonal climate among educators and their clientele.

A school's staff may agree to ask each teacher to make a certain number of telephone contacts each month for the next five months. In making these outreach efforts, the conversation might make the following emphasis:

> "Mrs. Jones, this is John's teacher calling. I wanted to give you a ring to get better acquainted and to let you know how much I appreciate having your son in my class this year.
>
> "Needless to say, anything you could tell me about John that would help me in my teaching would be appreciated.
>
> "Also, I have a few comments and suggestions for you. We need to work as closely as possible to encourage and motivate John to do his best in school."

A deliberate outreach initiative of this type from the child's teacher to the home will build bridges of communication and understanding. Unless an outreach effort is planned with some detailed action steps, many fine opportunities are missed.

An outreach objective that plans in detail how contacts are to be made will launch a school well on the way to increased effectiveness. By committing the school to follow MBO procedures in executing a master plan to reach more homes and more parents, the efficiency of this vital function will be greatly enhanced.

Parent Volunteers

Individualized instruction is in greater demand and teacher loads are increasing today. A parent-volunteers objective will provide schools with a potential rich resource to decrease the work load on teachers. There are many tasks that need to be performed in today's schools that do not require professionally prepared competence.

More understanding, identification and commitment to a school's program will likely be another valuable byproduct of a parent-volunteers program. Additionally, teachers may be freed from routine tasks to devote more time to the teaching and learning process. Under the direction of teachers, some tutorial work and student assistance in individualized study may be possible through use of parent volunteers.

Careful preparation and orientation is necessary in a parent-volunteers program. Under the MBO system, action steps to recruit volunteers, attain consensus among teachers on how best to use the talents of volunteers, and training of all individuals to be involved can be executed. Problems can be anticipated and actions taken to solve them. Systematic follow-through and evaluation of the program can be worked into the operational planning process.

Under the careful control and deliberate development that is inherent in all well-designed and executed MBO programs, a parent-volunteers program will be a truly productive effort to enhance learning and help in some measure to solve the teacher load problem that exists in the schools of the Granite School District.

Appendix D

**Instructions, Time-Phased Action Step Chart,
and Accompanying Forms Used in
Granite School District MBO System**

GRANITE SCHOOL DISTRICT

340 EAST 3545 SOUTH • *SALT LAKE CITY, UTAH 84115*

Telephone (801)

AN INTRODUCTION TO GRANITE SCHOOL DISTRICT
MANAGEMENT BY OBJECTIVES PROJECT

1. Benefits Derived from an MBO Program

   Management by objectives is an approach to making the planning and execution
   of school operations more universally understood by all school staff members
   and to encourage the staff to focus more attention to outputs and results.
   An MBO system, if properly implemented with involvement of the staff, should
   create a sense of unity and teamwork in the school. Results oriented management assures the staff that the school is aware of its problems and is concentrating on solutions. It generates interest because progress is well known,
   and this sense of momentum causes enthusiasm.

2. Plans for Initial Learning Experience

   The Granite School District will initiate some first steps in gaining some of
   the positive benefits from MBO during the school year. This will be
   a learning experience, and only a limited number of objectives will be adopted
   for deliberate management to accomplishment as we learn what MBO is all
   about. Hopefully, this will prepare us for the next year when a more fully
   implemented effort can be launched.

3. Performance Priorities Suggested by the Superintendent

   Each year the Superintendent will suggest some performance priorities that
   reflect some district-wide needs. These may not, however, be the most
   urgent educational needs of a particular school. Each school should consider
   these performance priorities carefully but other priorities should also be
   considered. The Principal and his staff should set the objectives to be
   included as MBO system targets for the year. This should be done, however,
   after careful consideration of district-wide priorities.

   As an initial experience it is recommended that three top priority objectives
   be adopted as school-wide educational outcomes. This does not mean that
   only these outcomes are important. It simply identifies the objectives to be
   systematically pursued as a learning experience in attaining expertise in
   MBO operations and as a means of setting and striving to attain some highly
   desirable school goals.

GRANITE SCHOOL DISTRICT
340 EAST 3545 SOUTH • SALT LAKE CITY, UTAH 84115
Telephone (801)

GRANITE SCHOOL DISTRICT OPERATIONAL PLANNING SYSTEM
AND MANAGEMENT BY OBJECTIVES PROGRAM

MBO FORM A --Statement of Objectives and of Related Sub-Objectives

1. Problem Description

    Describe in concise language the educational problem to be solved. Try to
    quantify the problem with objective data. Be as brief as possible, and use
    words to describe without resorting to jargon. Use plain and descriptive
    language.

Administrative Complex _____ School_____Page #_____

GRANITE SCHOOL DISTRICT

340 EAST 3545 SOUTH • SALT LAKE CITY, UTAH 84115
Telephone (801

(SUPPLEMENTAL INFORMATION TO ACCOMPANY MBO FORM A)

2. Statement of Major Objective

Try to state in measurable terms the outcome to be attained. Be sure to express the outcome in time phase so that a time certain is known when the objective will be accomplished. Describe the distance between what is and what will be if the objective is accomplished. Be sure to describe the objective in realistic terms. Do not over-aspire nor state an outcome that cannot realistically be sought with the resources available. It is helpful to remember that MBO planning is output oriented. Express the results to be attained.

Administrative Complex_____ School_____ Page #_____

GRANITE SCHOOL DISTRICT

340 EAST 3545 SOUTH • SALT LAKE CITY, UTAH 84115

Telephone (801)

(SUPPLEMENTAL INFORMATION TO ACCOMPANY MBO FORM A)

3. Statement of Sub-Objective

Some objectives are large and complex. To be attained, a number of
significant goals must be reached in order for a substantive outcome to
be reached. Using the guidelines expressed for describing a major objective,
put down a description of sub-objectives if such are needed to outline the
outcomes sought. (Some objectives will not require statements of sub-objectives
and Section 3 of Form A will not be needed in many operational plans.)

GRANITE SCHOOL DISTRICT

340 EAST 3545 SOUTH • SALT LAKE CITY, UTAH 84115
Telephone (801)

Name of School_____

Administrative Complex_____

Principal_____

MBO Form B--Time Phased Action Steps to Attain Major Objectives or
Significant Sub-Objectives
(To be used to monitor progress in MBO)

In the form below list the detailed action steps to be executed in accomplishing the objective or sub-objective. The following symbols will denote beginning dates and completion dates for each action step:

④————————————————/13\

O = month and day action step is initiated.

△ = month and day action step is completed.

———————— = the line shows the duration of activity from initiation to completion.

Action Steps	Staff Member Responsible	M O N T H S												Explanation and more detail on page # attached
		J	A	S	O	N	D	J	F	M	A	M	J	

Page #

GRANITE SCHOOL DISTRICT
340 EAST 3545 SOUTH • SALT LAKE CITY, UTAH 84115
Telephone (801)

(SUPPLEMENTAL INFORMATION TO ACCOMPANY MBO FORM B)

Detailed Explanation of Action Step and How the Same Will be Accomplished

Describe in sufficient detail to provide information on how the school plans to complete the time-phased activity as part of the total plan in accomplishing the objective outlined in MBO Form A.

Administrative Complex_____School_____Page #____

Index